Not Many Wise Are Called

A Missionary Couple's Journal:
Forty Years of Ministry to Latin America

By: Kenneth and Deany Lowry

PRESS

Not Many Wise Are Called
A Missionary Couple's Journal: Forty Years of Ministry
to Latin America
by Kenneth and Deany Lowry

Printed in the United States of America

ISBN 978-1-60647-693-2

www.xulonpress.com

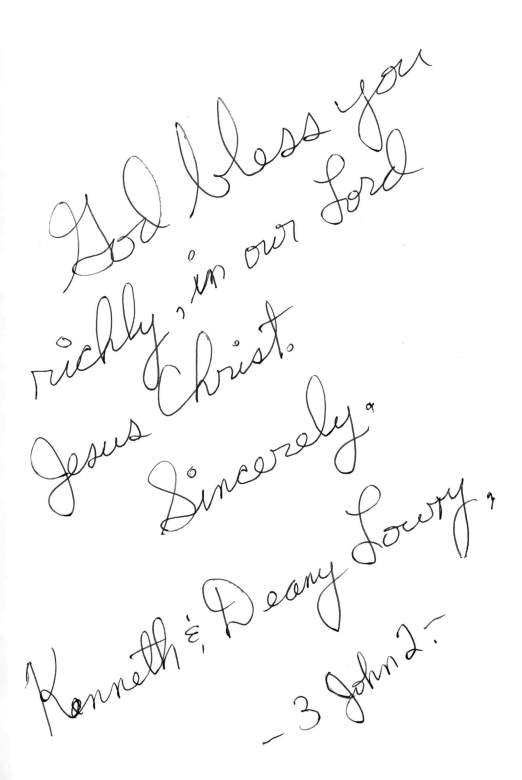

God bless you richly, in our Lord Jesus Christ.

Sincerely,

Kenneth & Deany Lowry,

—3 John 2—

"I'm Coming Stanley"

Photo Legend:

January, 1968. Kenneth Lowry at the age of 32 packed and ready for his first missionary journey to Oaxaca, South Mexico.

"I'm Coming, Stanley" is a humorous quote from David Livingston to the English reporter, Mr. Stanley, who was sent to find the lost missionary. When Livingston learned that the reporter was searching for him, he sent word – "I'm Coming, Stanley".

DEDICATION

This missionary autobiography is dedicated to Deany Lowry, my wife of 51 years, a midwife of over 25 years and a lifetime friend of 52 years. Without her, this book would not have been made possible.

Also, this dedication extends to our 5 children, their spouses, 16 grandchildren and 3 great-grandchildren.

Kenneth W. Lowry

INTRODUCTION OF AUTHOR

In this age of technology, our generation has more information available to them than any other, yet one thing lacking in our society today is the wisdom that is passed down from one generation to another. We must learn to tap into the reservoirs of wisdom available to us from our elders. One such reservoir is Kenneth Lowry, a good friend and mentor of mine for many years.

Kenneth said something I'll never forget when I was first ordained into the ministry, before I entered into full time ministry. After the ordination, he took me aside and said, "Manuel, remember, your calling comes first, then your job. Don't be afraid to give up your job for your calling." Many years later, those words were an inspiration to me when I had to make a decision of letting go of my day job and entering into full-time ministry.

The irony of the title to this book, "Not Many Wise Are Called", is that you will find much wisdom and experience from a man who dared to believe God and venture out to live a life of faith.

Manuel B. Montez
Senior Pastor, Iglesia Vida de Pacto

With deep gratitude to Him Who
calls and sustains His "called-out
ones", this autobiography of our
missionary years in Latin America is also
dedicated to all who serve as home
and foreign missionaries.

Sincerely,

Kenneth & Deany Lowry
15 February 2003

PREFACE

First of all, Deany, our family and I are extremely grateful to all the named and unnamed people who have encouraged us to do the work of a missionary family in Latin America.

We lived in Guadalajara, Jalisco, Mexico in 1972 – 1973. Later we lived in San Pedro Sula, Honduras, Central America from 1973 – 1976.

We definitely enjoyed all the aspects of missionary endeavors, such as T.V., radio, newspaper articles, city-wide evangelistic crusades, church and home meetings, training others for the ministry, and our own family life together in different countries. Our family became very close as we traveled back and forth together to the States. They still talk about living as a family outside of the United States and how this deeply enriched their lives.

We gratefully acknowledge David Love for typing the original doctoral manuscript.

Finally, Deany and I want to personally thank Mrs. Diane Noriega for putting this doctoral manuscript into story form for our friends, family and new friends who read this book; "Not Many Wise Are Called".

May you experience some of the thrills, tears and laughter that we experienced as missionaries in Latin America. God bless you richly!

Sincerely

Kenneth & Deany Lowry
III John 2

KEN LOWRY'S LATIN AMERICAN MINISTRY
An Autobiography

"For you see your calling, brethren, how that
NOT MANY WISE MEN AFTER THE FLESH,
NOT MANY MIGHTY,
NOT MANY NOBLE ARE CALLED."

1 Corinthians 1:26

Submitted By:
Kenneth W. Lowry

Liberty Theological Seminary

D.P. Min. Graduate Degree Program

Professor Frank Longino, Dr. C.E.

Final Paper

July 7, 1997

Chapter 1

THE EARLY YEARS
(1935-1971)

I was born on February 20, 1935 in a clapboard house on five acres of land that backed up into the woods, a mile and a half outside of the Houston, Texas city limits. Those were the depression years preceding WWII and we didn't have much in the way of the world's goods, but none of our neighbors did either. I enjoyed all the privileges of being born the fourth son of George and Myrtie Lowry in the middle of the Great Depression. The baggy, hand-me-down clothes gave me good reason to grow. We had everything that we needed: our two bedroom house, an outside water pump, a two-seater outhouse, a large vegetable garden, a milk cow, and lots of chickens. We attended the Rosalyn Road Baptist Church across from Turkey Gulley, where my brothers and I learned to swim. I caught impetigo from sharing the creek with the local cows. Daddy took the pickup to work, which left us walking a mile to catch the bus or riding our bicycles everywhere we went.

One day, when I was six years old, I felt strongly that I would be a missionary to Africa. When nobody was looking, I would stand in front of the mirror in my parents' room and pretend I was a preacher. Later I practiced my preaching on chickens as I scattered their feed. When I was 11 years old, in 1946, I publicly accepted Jesus Christ as my Savior. I later understood that this was a spiritual conception, but my actual new birth came twenty years later, when I was thirty-one. At the age of thirteen I began evangelizing my friends. I did not exactly know the definition of evangelism. I would wrestle with my buddy, Orville McNabb, as we rolled around in a ditch with my hands on his package of cigarettes - and he with his hands around my throat. I was really trying to evangelize him. Initially I was not too successful with my efforts in evangelizing the lost, but I kept at it anyway. Another early "ministerial" experience I had was with my brother's friend, Joe Lee Box. I would arrive at his house early on Sunday mornings in order to pour tomato juice down his throat to help him become sober before taking the one mile walk with him to the Garden Oaks Baptist Church. In 1948 the new pastor, Brother James W. Parker, resembled Johnny Weissmuller, "Tarzan", in the movies. I would invite my buddies to come to church with me and see "Tarzan" behind the pulpit.

In November of 1948, Evangelist Oral Roberts erected a revival tent across the road from our pasture where my brothers and I parked cars for fifty cents each. After parking all the cars, we went to the services. I got in the healing line one night. When it came my turn to be prayed over, Brother Roberts asked me what I needed. Breathing heavily, I told him I needed to be healed from bronchitis and asthma. He laid his hands on me and prayed. Ten years later when I was in theological seminary, I overheard several students working on their doctor of theology degrees discussing that Oral Roberts was a hoax. I told them my story, and that I no longer had asthma. Over the years Oral Roberts and Billy Graham have been my two heroes.

After graduating from Houston's Reagan High School at 17, I worked in the Merchant Marines from 1952-53 to save money for college. I sent all my earnings home to be saved by my parents. Because of the financial needs at home - my brother in medical school, and two younger sisters, the money had been borrowed when I was ready to go to college. However, the money I lent my family was repaid during my seminary years. I worked the summer of 1953 at Mr. Campbell's grocery store, and in August, a friend took me to the University of Texas in Austin to enroll as a freshman. I studied basic pre-medical courses and a speech therapy class to help overcome stuttering. Early one morning while studying for a biology quiz, the Lord spoke to me and said, "You are going to be a preacher." I didn't see how being a public speaker could ever happen because of my speech impediment, but I was willing!

HARDIN-SIMMONS UNIVERSITY AND MARRIAGE

The following year I transferred to Hardin-Simmons University in Abilene, Texas and remained there until graduating three years later. H-SU is a small, Southern Baptist university. I was able to attend through a scholarship given by Dr. Joe Redden of the Garden Oaks Baptist Church in Houston. It was at H-SU that I met my future wife, the former Deany Gandy. She was a student at Hendrick's College of Nursing, located a block from the university campus. My dad always told me to get my education before I married. I followed his instructions. The day following graduation on May 31, 1957, we were married in the chapel of Abilene's First Baptist Church.

SOUTHWESTERN SEMINARY DAYS

Upon graduation from Hardin-Simmons, we moved to Southwestern Baptist Theological Seminary in Fort Worth, Texas, to study for the next four years. Deany attended the Harris College of Nursing in Fort Worth, but was forced to leave during her second year because of health problems.

In 1958, my second year in seminary, I received a call to be pastor of Marystown Baptist Church near Cleburne, Texas. Following that position, we moved to Dallas where I was youth pastor and Deany was church secretary at Trinity Baptist. Also during this time, I was a YMCA director and a juvenile group worker at the Dallas County Juvenile Detention Center. On the weekends, I pastored the Rock Bluff Baptist Church near Gorman, Texas, 150 miles southwest of Dallas. By the time I graduated, I was really tired.

FIRST FULL-TIME PASTORATE

In 1961 I graduated from seminary and we moved to the panhandle of Texas where I pastored the Lesley Baptist Church. Deany, due to many sleepless nights from caring for twin babies, developed a strong depression, causing a nervous breakdown. (She was delivered from a spirit of depression in 1967). I also needed deliverance from the spirit of pornographic mental pictures. The need for freedom of this tormenting spirit drove me to talk to Pastor Glenn Bailey who had spoken to our congregation. That Sunday afternoon I shared with him the problem that I had been trying to overcome for several years. Because I wanted to be as pure as Christ, this problem was a "thorn in my flesh." After confessing to Brother Glenn, he put his hands on my head and asked the Lord to deliver me. I felt really cleansed after his prayer.

While we were still with the Lesley Baptist Church we had our first crusade with the migrant workers from Mexico. In 1961-62, George Arthur, pastor of nearby Brice Baptist Church, and I led seventy-five Mexicans to accept Jesus and be water baptized. Later George started an African-American church in Brice and I pastored a Mexican church nearby in Memphis, as well as the anglo congregation in Lesley, Texas.

GOD MEANS BUSINESS

In 1976 while living back in Houston, occasionally I took my boys to the woods to hunt whatever we could find, such as squirrels, rabbits, possums or snakes. Dan and David had BB guns; Steve had a knife tied to a long stick, James just had a stick, while I carried a pellet gun. As each one of us was going a different trail, I stopped by a trash pile in the woods and noticed a Playboy magazine. I picked it up, and as I was trying to open the rain-soaked, sun-dried pages, I noticed four little boys watching me. I lied to cover my embarrassment, and said, "I just wanted to see if these magazines were as bad as they used to be." God is so good to expose us in order to help men to be godly daddies! This episode really helped me to get further deliverance from a carnal mindset.

WESTWAY BAPTIST CHURCH

From Lesley, we moved near Hereford, Texas, Deany's hometown, where I was pastor of the Westway Baptist Church during 1962-

63. Here I learned to drive a school bus and to work with a younger church fellowship. At this church we had several good revival meetings among the people. Steve, our middle son, was born during this pastorate. Early one Sunday morning, Deany and I were disagreeing about taking the family to church because Steve was sick. As I was angrily driving alone the three miles to the church service, the Lord spoke to me saying, "Deany, first of all is My daughter; secondly, she is your sister; and thirdly, she is your wife." My understanding had it backwards. However I have never forgotten the order He gave me that Sunday morning in 1962.

WALLER BAPTIST CHURCH

The last denominational church I pastored was the Waller Baptist Church, 40 miles west of Houston. We were there for over three years, from 1963-1967. The Lord added sixty-six new members during my first year as pastor. Thirty-three came by conversion and water baptism. We had two revivals and a youth revival every year, as well as church visitation twice each week. James, our youngest son, was born while I pastored in Waller. It was during this time that we applied to the Foreign Mission Board of the Southern Baptist Convention as missionary candidates to French West Africa. The biggest task required of us by the Foreign Mission Board was to write our complete autobiographies.

REJECTIONS HURT

Due to health reasons, we were not accepted by the Board as overseas missionaries. Besides Deany's earlier nervous breakdown, Steve had asthmatic bronchitis and James had just been hospitalized with viral meningitis. Not being able to accomplish my life's goal as a missionary caused me to experience depression much similar to that of a divorced person who is rejected by his spouse. (However, this experience gave me compassion for divorced people. Previously I did not understand the hurt that divorced people felt).

Later that same year on a Sunday afternoon the Lord told me to preach on the "race issue." I said, "No way! Waller County is 76%

African-American." The Lord said, "If you don't, you will have stuttering speech again." I said, "Yes, Lord, I will preach on the race issue!" The message I preached that evening was "How to Be Filled With the Holy Spirit." I've preached literally thousands of sermons in forty-five years of ministry, but of all those sermons, this is one I have never forgotten. The sermon outline was this:

I   To be filled with the Holy Spirit, a person must not quench the Spirit by feeling superior to others.

II   To be filled with the Holy Spirit, a person must not grieve the Spirit by rejecting other people.

III.   To be filled with the Holy Spirit, a person must honor all people, regardless of race and position in life.

After the service only seven people shook my hand. The remainder of the congregation exited the building through side doors because they were upset with the message. I was so discouraged that night that when I went to bed I pulled the sheet over my head and told the Lord that I had fought a good fight and that I had kept the faith; hopefully there would be a crown laid up for me in Glory. "So Lord, please take me home – I'm ready." The next morning as I looked out from under the sheets, I knew I wasn't in heaven. The furniture there would have been much better than what I was seeing in our bedroom. No one called that day and I felt very lonely. I began to make plans that afternoon to drive to Houston, to eat a big Mexican meal, drink a large root beer and go to a movie. (This was a pattern for me when I felt depressed). However, my plans were interrupted on Monday at 4:45 p.m., when the church building caught fire. The ten dollar bill in my office which I had planned to spend that evening was destroyed by the devastating fire along with everything else.

ARTHUR B. RUTLEDGE
Executive Secretary-Treasurer

HOME MISSION BOARD
SOUTHERN BAPTIST CONVENTION
161 SPRING STREET, N. W., ATLANTA, GEORGIA 30303 TELEPHONE: CODE 404 523-2593

DEPARTMENT OF MISSIONARY PERSONNEL
• GLENDON McCULLOUGH, Secretary

April 11, 1966

Rev. Kenneth W. Lowry
Waller Baptist Church
Waller, Texas 77484

Dear Mr. Lowry:

Please let me thank you for your letter of April 1. I am very sorry to know that you have gone through this disappointment of not being able to serve abroad as you had felt lead to do.

Whether or not you could be appointed by the Home Mission Board would depend upon our completing a file. Some of this file the Foreign Mission Board can share with us if you authorize it. Our first procedure would be to ask you to write the Personnel Department, authorizing the release of confidential information in your file. If the reasons for being declined did not seem to be reasons that would effect the service in the continental United States, we would proceed in working with you to complete a file for possible appointment by the Home Mission Board.

We have an agreement with the Foreign Mission Board to share any information concerning a file, but we do not transfer these files from one Board to another. We would need to get essentially the same file that they have for appointment by the Home Mission Board.

I do not know what the possibilities are for work among the Negroes in Texas. We would engage in work there as requested by the state convention, and this would be through the office of Dr. Paul Aiken, who is director of the work with National Baptists in the state of Texas. You might want to contact him regarding possibilities in your area.

I will be happy to be of any assistance that I can. Be assured of our prayers as you continue to seek to find and to follow the Lord's will for your lives.

Sincerely yours,

Glendon McCullough

GM:ed

THE BAPTISM IN THE HOLY SPIRIT

On June 26, 1966 I was so discouraged from the rejections of the Foreign Mission Board and our local Baptist congregation, that I went to see Pastor Tommy Phelps at the Temple Baptist Church in Hereford, Texas. I told him I didn't know if I was lost or saved. After he ministered to me through Scripture and prayer, I have never doubted my salvation for one second. In December of 1966 after the new church building was rebuilt, the Lord sent a Pentecostal evangelist and a spirit-filled, former Baptist "home missionary," to pray for me in Waller. While sitting on the front row of that beautiful, new sanctuary, the Baptist minister laid his hands on my head and prayed for me to receive the baptism of the Holy Spirit. After arguing scriptures with these two men, Bob Buess and F.E. Ward, I finally understood these Old Testament and New Testament scriptures and received the Baptism of the Holy Spirit with the evidence of speaking in a heavenly language. Besides salvation and sanctification, this has been the most meaningful experience I've ever known.

A SIGNIFICANT HEALING

Several months later, while in a prayer meeting with a Baptist deacon and a Methodist minister, the Lord told me to anoint and pray for Margie Blackford, and He would heal her. Margie was suffering with cirrhosis of the liver which was caused by contaminated seafood. She had been sent home by her doctors to die. I argued with the Lord, saying, "I can't pray for her; she's a member of our Baptist church." At this time I didn't want anyone in the church to know I was a Charismatic because it did not agree with our Baptist teachings. I didn't mind praying for the Pentecostals, and others who came through our town, but I was trying to keep my new experience private. I took Pastor Robert Parks of the Weslayan Methodist Church with me to pray for Margie. He prayed, "If it's Your will Lord, heal Margie." But since the Lord told me to go pray for Margie, I knew it was His will to heal her. I anointed her with oil and prayed, "Margie Blackford, be thou made whole in the name of Jesus," and we left her house. Three days later Margie was feeling so well, she was able to do her house work and attend church services. Later, however, her friends and relatives talked her into taking her medicine again and going back to bed. Soon afterwards, Margie passed away.

KEEPING OUR VOWS

I made a vow with the Lord that as soon as my wife was baptized in the Holy Spirit, I would leave the pastorate and become a full-time evangelist. Three months later, in March of 1967, we were teaching a Bible lesson at the home of charismatic Presbyterians, Mac and Ada Ruth Boyd. That evening following the Bible study, Judy Hester and Bernice Schmidt prayed for Deany to receive the baptism in the Holy Spirit. She soon began to speak in her own heavenly language. I had forgotten my vow with the Lord, but He didn't. Two months later, during a pastor/deacons' meeting, it was decided that I should resign as pastor of the Waller Baptist Church because of this Pentecostal experience. Keeping my vow to become an evangelist when my wife received the baptism in the Holy Spirit has been a great blessing over these past thirty-plus years, as the Lord has allowed me to minister as a missionary-evangelist in almost forty countries around the world.

MY FIRST WINE COMMUNION

As a Southern Baptist, we never used real wine for a communion service - only grape juice. Was I surprised when I took communion with Pastor Joseph Castleman's charismatic Church of Christ fellowship in San Antonio one Sunday morning in 1967! Brother F.E. Ward had warned me that this church used wine for communion, but still I was startled as this strong beverage went down my throat. Without debating the issue, I realized for the first time that wine was most likely the drink used by the early church for communion services.

MY FIRST FOOT WASHING

During an evening service in Jack and Dorothy Gibson's home in Austin, Texas, we had both a communion and a foot washing service. Since this was my first foot washing experience, I was so overwhelmed with the love of God that I actually wept and literally kissed the brother's feet that I was washing. The next morning Jack asked me how much the Lord was giving me each month as a salary. I humbly said, "Almost $500 each month." He then laid hands on me and prayed, "In the name of Jesus Christ, I command a raise for Kenneth of $250 per month." Within two months my salary increased to $750 per month. Wow! I was learning that the Lord really wants to bless us through our own faith and also through the corporate faith of the body of Christ.

FULL-GOSPEL BUSINESSMEN'S FELLOWSHIP

In July of 1967, we left the pastorate and found a house in Houston for Deany, myself, Dan, David, Steve and James. I began traveling and giving my testimony with the Full Gospel Businessmen's Fellowship in Texas, and later across the south and northeastern United States. On one of these trips to Baker, Louisiana, during a revival meeting with Roy Stockstill, I learned about praying deliverance for people who were depressed. When I returned to Houston, several of us prayed and ministered deliverance to Deany, so she would be freed from a spirit of depression. Following her deliverance Deany exclaimed, "I feel younger and lighter than I have in a long time."

CALM DOWN, SON

Bill and Celeste Brunner, who befriended us, also helped us find a house in the Spring Branch area of West Houston. We have lived here for 30 years except when we were missionaries in Mexico and Central America. After we had moved into our house, one morning while shaving, I asked the Lord to give me one hand for healing the sick like Oral Roberts and the other hand for inviting people to come to know Jesus, like Billy Graham (I wanted to serve the Lord so much). The Lord spoke to me and said, "Son, you'd make me nervous if you could. How would you like your children to bounce on the bed every morning, saying, "Dad, we want to do this and that and the other?" Don't confuse activity and busy-ness as serving the Lord".

LEARNING TO LIVE BY FAITH ONE DAY AT A TIME

While traveling and preaching, Deany kept reminding me that the roof leaked in our newly acquired house. Finally, I got up enough nerve to tackle the job. Since we only had forty dollars to spend on the roof, I bought a box of nails and several squares of shingles. Bill Brunner came over to help with the roofing. Every time we needed more shingles, the Lord would send more money. After a week of roofing, we finished the job and the flow of extra money ceased. This, as well as similar experiences, helped me to develop a dependency on the Lord as my Provider.

FIRST MISSIONARY ADVENTURES

In February of 1968, my first missionary trip was with John Crawford and Doug Messel to the state of Oaxaca, in southern Mexico. I ministered with Greely Pannell in a Catholic Seminary near Toronto, Canada, in October of 1969. The following summer, Ray Wallace, Ed Tallant and I preached in Braes River, St. Elizabeth, Jamaica. More and more, I was beginning to feel fulfillment in doing what the Lord had called me to do as a six-year-old boy. Months later in 1971, Deany, James and I traveled with Jim and Helen Mann in their motor home to La Democracia, Guatemala, in Central America, to hold a crusade with Missionary Norman Parish. My hunger to be a full-time missionary was very intense at this time. I really yearned to live on the mission field with my family. In the summer of 1972, we left our house in the care of our good friends Samuel and Sheryl Freeze, and moved our family to Guadalajara, Mexico, to become full-time missionaries. However, we had financial fears: money for our four sons' schooling; money for language school for Deany and me; money for living expenses for the six of us; etc. But over a period of time, the Lord helped us overcome these human fears and to depend on Him to meet our every need.

ELEVEN DAYS IN MEXICO
(Five days in San Mateo)

On February 29, 1968, John Crawford, Douglas Messel and I flew from Houston, Texas, to Veracruz, Mexico. (Eight months before, God had spoken to me and had told me to go to Mexico.) During a layover, God directed us to meet Missionary F.L. Thornton. After prayer, Brother Thornton felt led to drive us 500 miles to Huixtla, near the border of Guatemala. We stopped in Juchitan Friday night, and met Roberto Salizar and Missionary Jene McDonald. That same night we held services in La Ventosa, and saw God stop the next-door tavern music, save two Indians, fill several more with the Holy Spirit and heal others.

We left Saturday for Huixtla and, after good fellowsip with Missionaries Ken and Fran Ulfeng, returned to Juchitan. Roberto Salizar had received prophecy that some men would arrive to accompany them to San Mateo. A year previously, God used him to pray for a man who had been dead for eleven hours, and God raised him up. Since then, revival had continuously broken out in Juchitan and eight other places.

Monday: Services began as we played a T.L. Osborn tape. We were met by all the drunks of the town. We retreated into our hut and prayed.

Tuesday: We went from house-to-house, witnessing about Jesus and leaving tracts.

Wednesday: A lady tried to run us out of the hut we were staying in. (Friday morning, she accepted Jesus as her Savior.) Four men accepted Christ, two others healed, and we ate supper with the Roman Catholic priest of San Mateo. That night we had a sing-song service, with about 25 children.

Thursday: We went to Santa Maria and met Narviso Alvares, who was put into prison twelve years before for preaching the Gospel. Two years before, he and another Christian prayed for a man at 11:00 A.M., and at 12:00 midnight, God raised him from the dead. (He had been dead for three days.) After this, the town elected Narciso as their mayor, and revival broke out in Santa Maria. God directed Civilo Garcia, a Huave Indian preacher, to meet us in Santa Maria. He returned with us to San Mateo, and the town had its first street service at which God saved 22 people that night and healed others.

Friday: We returned to Tehuantapec and had services with Renaldo Trugillo in his new building, which was provided through the Native Ministry Crusade of Gordon Lindsey and Wayne Myers.

Saturday: On the bus, God saved a Latin American who had lived in San Antonio. At supper, a man from Houston accepted Christ. Later that night, a couple from Oregon accepted Jesus as Savior.

Sunday: In Brother Thornton's Pentecostal Church of God School, we saw seven people baptized in the Holy Spirit with the evidence of speaking in a "heavenly language". The young preacher's father, who was saved two weeks earlier, also received the baptism.

Monday: We arrived back in Houston, praising the Lord!

LIVE AND LEARN

I came back from one missionary trip to Southern Mexico with blisters on every one of my toes. Seeing the poverty of some of the Mexican Christians, I gave away all of my extra clothes and shoes. I bought a cheap pair of sandals that didn't fit my feet, thus causing the blisters. Later, when Deany traveled with me, she took better care of me.

Chapter 2

GUADALAJARA, MEXICO
(1972-1973)

GETTING STARTED IN MISSIONS

B efore moving to Mexico, Jack Morris and I made several missionary trips into Mexico, including the states of Oaxaca, Jalisco, Nayarit, Vera Cruz, San Luis Potosi and others. One of the trips we made between 1969 and 1972 (which is especially vivid in my memory) was the trip to Tepic, where we ministered in the "badlands" to the Huechole Indians. Many murders had been committed due to family feuds. There was a Baptist orphanage in the area where widows and children lived.

After ministering at the orphanage, we were invited to spend the night. We slept on the benches in the small church auditorium. Hordes of fleas soon drove us outside, where we slept in and on Jack's 1970 Ford station wagon. I was blessed on this trip to see the beans which we were to eat before they were cooked. All of the beans I saw had holes in them, so I decided to go on a fast. Some of the others had trouble with diarrhea because the beans were really bad.

MISSIONARY ZEAL

After many such missionary trips, I became restless in Houston, having tasted the foreign mission field and the openness of third-world peoples to receive the gospel of Christ. We tried to sell our house and then lease it, without success. Finally, we rented the house to Samuel and Sheryl Freeze and their two children who lived in it for the next four years while we lived in Mexico and Honduras. They were so helpful in depositing missionary funds that we could withdraw, as well as forwarding our mail to us. About this time, Warren Crane, Jr., a Spirit-filled Catholic brother, gave us a 1970 Chevrolet Blazer and a 1965 Shasta trailer which we loaded and took to Mexico with our four children.

THE JOURNEY BEGINS

As we left Houston, Ray and Jestilene Wallace from Prattville, Alabama, traveled with us as far as El Paso to encourage us. People had promised to help us with about $90-$120 per month, but I had butterflies in my stomach about how we were going to make it financially. I preached in the El Paso area to have more money before moving to Mexico. The Lord was in the process of teaching me how to live by faith - not faith in people, but faith in His ability to provide for the ones He has called. Over the weeks and months my faith began to grow.

ON THE ROAD THROUGH MEXICO

As we traveled through Mexico, I taught our boys how to drop tracts out the windows of the Blazer. One boy must look behind to see if another car or truck is following. The "tract dropper" must look ahead to see if any cars or trucks are approaching us. If the coast is clear, a tract is dropped about 10 yards in front of people walking along the highway. We have seen several new church buildings planted along the Mexican highways as a result of people being converted to Christ who read the gospel tracts. Some missionary statistics concerning Mexico indicate that every newspaper or gospel tract is read at least seven times by different people.

ON THE MISSION FIELD

When we arrived in Ciudad Granja (near Guadalajara), we lived in our 18' Shasta trailer for six weeks. The boys didn't even want to come inside to eat because the trailer was so confining. Regardless of how we moved, we were always in someone else's way. After the six week initiation, we were blessed to stay in Pat Pride's large house near the police station for the following month. We had to make friends with his half shepherd, half coyote dog that guarded the house. For the rest of the year while I was in language school, we paid $65 per month to rent a three-bedroom, tiled house, with a beautiful rose garden in front. We had planned to home-school the boys, but the books we ordered from Chicago never arrived; they probably got lost somewhere in the Mexican post office. The Lord provided a tutor from California who taught the boys for six weeks.

FEELING WEAK

One day while Deany and I were in language school, and the boys were at the tutor's house, she became ill and sent the boys home on the bus. Dan, David and Steve jumped off the bus as it slowed down and continued running. But James, the youngest, at age 7, didn't know that he was to continue running after he jumped, so he fell flat on his face. He received cuts above and below the left eye, which bled profusely. Pat Pride called me at language school, telling me to come to the clinic immediately to see if James needed stitches. As the doctor sewed up the two cuts, I almost passed out due to the heat and heart-wrenching pain I felt for James. After this experience we put our four boys in the school for missionary children, which was adjacent to the language school.

UPTIGHT IN SCHOOL

We went to language school because Pat Pride, a missionary friend, told me that my high school Spanish was "awful." This happened just after I showed gospel films in nearby villages with missionaries Jim Pursifull and Byron Hunter. So I decided that Deany and I should go to language school, while the boys were in private school. I studied Spanish five hours a day, five days a week, and four hours at home each night. Deany took a two-hour course three days a week from a nearby business school. As a result, we were always happy for holidays, which were numerous in Mexico. During this time of language schooling, Paul and Louise Storey sent their 19 year-old daughter, Linda, to live with us. She was a fine young lady, but I felt responsible for her since young Mexican men were noticing her. That situation, plus language school, helped make me somewhat "uptight."

AROUND THE MOUNTAIN ON HORSEBACK

Paul and Jesse Jones, American missionaries, had started a work in the mountains, which was a 12-hour trip on horseback, or 15 minutes by airplane. One day I made the trip to the mission on horseback with Paul and four other men. As we slowly spiraled up the mountainside in the hot sun, I almost fell off the horse when it ducked under a branch which I didn't see. This completely caught me off guard, but definitely woke me up as I looked straight down about 1,500 feet to where I would have fallen. The projector and film for the service came with the airplane after we arrived at the mission atop the mountain. We had a wonderful service that night, and traveled back home the next day. My backside felt abused by the horse, and I'm sure it had the same impression about me. When the trip was over, I was so glad to arrive safely at home and sleep in my own bed.

PRIDE AND GENEROSITY

One day I received two checks in the mail, one for $150 and the other for $50. Pat Pride came over to the trailer as I was studying and asked me to pray for his finances. I gave him the $50 check, but while praying the Holy Spirit told me to give him the $150 check. However, I was too proud to ask him to return the $50 check. He must have thought I was pretty "well off" for a missionary. I told Deany what "we" had done, (I always use the word "we" if I'm about to get in trouble) and she was not impressed because we were completely out of groceries. We didn't have anything to eat that night, but God provided for us through another couple, the Ralph Madisons, who invited us to their house for supper. I can honestly say that it was one of the best meals we have ever eaten in our lives.

DOMESTIC DETAILS

Some of Deany's recollections of Mexico include the butane water heater, which we lit every time we needed hot water. Water ran through the coils, thereby heating the water. However, the heater couldn't be left on all the time due to a possible fire hazard. Another memory was washing clothes, which was a real challenge even under normal circumstances for a family of six. When we moved into the adobe house, Paul and Jesse Jones lent us a Maytag ringer-washer, so once a week found Deany on the patio in the back, washing clothes. Later we bought a little Hoover "wash and spin" from our missionary neighbors, David and Rita Booth.

THANKSGIVING DINNER

In November of 1972, the George Thackerys and the Elmer Hurleys came to see us enroute to Puerto Vallarta, on the Pacific coast, to visit their missionary relatives. Since this was the Thanksgiving holiday, Deany, the boys and I went with them to Puerta Vallarta. After we arrived, we bought a sailfish for 12 cents a pound and ate it for our Thanksgiving dinner. Later the boys wanted to go swimming at the nearby beach. I was so full of fried fish that I made them wait a little while. But they badgered me to go with them to "just jump in the water," but not "swim."

NO DROWNING TODAY

A storm the previous day had caused a strong undertow. As we jumped up and down we were soon carried out into the bay. One of the boys said he could not touch bottom. All of a sudden, three of my sons, along with a Mexican boy and another missionary's son were swept along with me out into the bay. I thought to myself, "Lord, if You don't save us, we're going to drown." (Later I learned that 40 people had drowned in this very spot the previous year). The second time I spoke out loud, "Lord, if You don't save us we're going to drown."

LORD JESUS, HELP!

By this time Steve, my middle son, was on my shoulders and I was bobbing up and down. He said, "That's alright, Daddy, I can see." This time as I was going up and down in the water, I was screaming as loud as I could, "Lord, Jesus Christ, HEEEELLLLPPPPP!!" Three American hippies jumped into the water, and I'm thinking, "Not them, Lord." He said, "Shut up and hang on." Since that moment, this boy from the East Texas woods has never been critical about the length of a man's hair. I was so grateful to the Lord that all of us were saved - especially the children! I had told the Lord that we were all going to be saved - or none of us would be saved. (I couldn't have lived with myself if I had only saved the one on my shoulders and let the rest drown).

PENITENTIARY MINISTRY

After returning from the Thanksgiving holiday trip, we investigated the possibility of ministering in the two state penitentiaries. One was the adult facility and the other was for the youth. Soon the penitentiaries opened for us to minister and show Christian films. We ministered on Saturday mornings to the youth, and Sunday afternoons to the adults. During one service in the adult penitentiary, someone stole and hid my tape recorder. The four of us who had been ministering went outside and started singing and making a lot of noise, until the guard came to ask us what we were doing. After telling him our tape recorder had been stolen, he went in and told the inmates that the men outside were not going to stop singing until the tape recorder was returned. In a few minutes, we had the tape recorder and were on our way.

DEGREES OF POVERTY

Outside the penitentiary, I was witnessing to Alberto, who owned a bread truck. We began talking about the hard times of our youth. I told him I understood what he was saying because we were poor, too. He responded, "Kenneth, it is one thing to be a poor Texan, and another thing to be a poor Mexican." I have never forgotten that I am rich just to be an American.

IGNORANCE IS BLISS

During another Sunday penitentiary service, Jay Wagner, Ross Berryman and I were told by the inmates that they were going to make "eunuchs" out of us with their rusty razorblades the next time we came back. We didn't see Ross for a long time because he understood Spanish much better than we did! When we saw Ross again, Jay asked him why he quit ministering at the jail with us. Ross explained what the inmates had said, but nothing had happened during the several months after the incident. (Sometimes it seems good not to know all the details involved with a second language). One inmate who had accepted the Lord was serving a 35-year sentence. The Lord chose him to be the chaplain of the "penitentiary church."

DEANY GOT MAD!

After living in Mexico for a few months, the city water pump broke down, and the town "experts" spent six weeks repairing it. After one month without water they finally fixed it, but it soon broke again for another two weeks. We had to haul water from downtown in a red-painted barrel (55-gallons). When the water level was near the bottom of the barrel, we let the boys bathe in it. The red paint came off and was tracked all over the tile floor! Deany, usually a patient mother, finally made a declaration into the heavens: "Lord, if we don't get water soon, I'm going back to Texas! "The Lord heard her prayer, and the next day the city water pump was fixed and we had water. (Romans 10:13 "Whosoever shall CALL upon the Lord shall be delivered").

UPSET CHILDREN

In Ciudad Granja, where we lived on the outskirts of Guadalajara, the officials controlled stray animals by throwing poisoned meat on the ground. Our dog was out walking with James and ate some of this poisoned meat and died. The boys were really upset, and that incident tarnished their impression of the Mexican "dog catcher" methods.

NOBODY'S TOO TOUGH

Maria del Carmen, the daughter of our landlord, Mr. Rodriguez, came to see us one day in tears. She told us that her South Carolinian, Marine Corps' husband had been put in jail for getting drunk and fighting. She wanted me to go talk to him. After prayer, he accepted Jesus as his Savior, and became a Christian. Later, she became a Christian as well. Now they are living somewhere in California, hopefully serving the Lord.

SEVEN POLICE CARS

Our next school break was in April, 1973, when we went again to Puerto Vallarta. I was sitting with my projector on top of another missionary's Suburban, in the process of showing T.L. Osborn gospel films on the side wall of a white pharmacy building, when seven police cars surrounded the crowd. Most of the other missionaries blended into the crowd, but three of us were apprehended for showing religious movies without a permit.

IN THE LOCAL JAIL

Down at the police station, the chief of police was threatening to put us in jail. But an anointing of boldness came over me, and I started preaching to him. However, an urgent telephone call revealed that an American tourist had suffered a heart attack. All seven police cars were away from the station, so Bill Miller and his Suburban were needed to pick up the tourist and take him to the hospital. We were all very glad to get out of the jail situation and pick up the tourist. The Chief of Police finally realized that he wasn't going to get any money from us. Also he was probably glad to get rid of me and my preaching. But he did say that we could come back any Sunday we desired and preach to the prisoners.

HONDURAS, HERE WE COME

Due to financial needs, I went to El Paso, Texas several times during the language school year to speak in churches in order to help keep my family in Mexico. After 10 months in school we realized that the Lord was going to send us somewhere else before our sons' next school year started in September. In Texas and in Louisiana that summer we received prophesies that the Lord was opening up a door of ministry for us in Honduras. In Louisiana some believers knew the Baptist missionary, Lesley Keyes, who worked in San Pedro Sula, Honduras. As we drove the five day, 2,200 mile trip through Mexico and Guatemala into Honduras, we were not prepared for the long delays at the border crossings. Also unexpected was the primitive beauty of Central America.

Chapter 3

SAN PEDRO SULA, HONDURAS
(1973-1974)

GETTING STARTED, FIRST YEAR

In 1971, Paul Rau, of Houston, and I made a trip through Mexico, Guatemala, Honduras and Salvador, Central America. I did not know at this time that I would later live in Honduras. But after language school, much prayer, and the prophetic words spoken over us, we were directed to Central America in August of 1973. We pulled the trailer with the Blazer - which had a generator strapped to the top. The Shasta trailer now began to look somewhat like an "Airstream" trailer, because the five bicycles on top gave it a rounded appearance.

MEXICO CITY TRAFFIC

The trip to San Pedro Sula, Honduras, with four active sons in the Blazer and the trailer in tow was adventure enough. But going through 5 o'clock (p.m.) traffic in Mexico City was more adventure than I ever wanted. It seemed like all 15 million people in Mexico City had either a car, bicycle, motorcycle, truck or horse and cart. The Lord provided two brothers from Texas to travel behind us all the way to Honduras, making sure we made the trip safely and got settled.

ARRIVAL IN HONDURAS

In five days we arrived at the border of Honduras, and on our first day in San Pedro Sula, we visited with a Southern Baptist missionary, Brother Lesley Keyes. By that same evening he had found us a house. This was a miracle, and another reassurance that we were supposed to be in San Pedro Sula.

A SCHOOL MIRACLE

We enrolled the boys in a private school that was geared to fit the American nine-month school schedule. This particular school prepared students to study in the colleges and universities in the United States. We had asked the Lord to give us an American-type school so our boys would not be put back into lower grades while they learned Spanish. This was our second confirmation that Honduras was where we were to be missionaries. I did not know how I could afford to send our four boys to such a nice, expensive school. The school needed a librarian and a school nurse. Deany filled those positions in exchange for our children's school expenses - the third demonstration that we were in the right place.

CHURCH AT THE HOUSE

I began to show Christian movies with the Foursquare and Mennonite churches, and was readily accepted by them. This was the fourth evidence that we were in God's will. The Rhineharts, Spirit-filled Catholics, lent us furniture to go into our rented house in Colonia Figurora, by the children's park on the edge of town. I began to show movies under our house on Sunday afternoons, when the Indian ladies went to the river near our house to wash their clothes. For the next two years we held meetings on the first floor of our two-story house, which rested on concrete columns.

WHEW, IS IT HOT!

The temperature in our bedroom often climbed to over 100 degrees during the daytime. At night the gnats came in through the screen if we had the light on in the bedroom. Sometimes, the outside temperature was so hot that my throat would constrict, and I could barely talk. If I could just say, "Jesus", it would help. The next step would be to begin "praying in the Spirit," [unknown tongues], and my energy level would start coming back [Jude 20]. We learned that most families had one air conditioner in one room as a cool haven. The Shasta trailer had a small unit, so that became our "cooling off" asylum.

HIDING BEHIND THE HOUSE

Our first converts were two teenage neighbor girls, Toni and Aida Miranda. One day as they helped me carry groceries up the mountain road to our house, I led them in a prayer of salvation, whereby they both gave their lives to Jesus Christ as their Savior. Since Deany was working five days a week in the school, I washed the clothes behind the house in our little Hoover washing machine, hoping no one would see me. The Honduran men would not have appreciated an American man doing "woman's work." One day while I was washing the clothes, Mark Werner, a Honduran-born American, came by to receive the baptism in the Holy Spirit on his twentieth birthday. Mark is now a prominent international lawyer in Honduras.

ENGLISH SERVICES

We began to meet for English services in the home of Mark's parents, Ray and Joan Warner. Joan and I began to pray for some of her neighbors which resulted in Emalena Munson getting healed, saved, baptized in water and filled with the Holy Spirit. I spent the rest of our first year in Honduras showing Christian movies in the villages and working with different independent and denominational missionaries.

A DIRTY NEEDLE

After we had settled into our ministry in Honduras, Deany, the boys and I went to the Social Services Center, along with many other people, to get a yellow fever vaccination. I saw James, our seven year-old son, punch a lady in the stomach. I was about to reprimand him when the lady said it was all right; she said she had been pinching his face because he had blond hair (which was a very uncommon sight in Honduras). After the vaccination, I came down with hepatitis-B because a contaminated needle was used. I was in bed for about six weeks. The only thing that really worked during those days in bed was my mind.

SLOW GOINGS

I would crawl out of bed to the bathroom, and then crawl back to the bed. Graciela, our maid, moved very slowly and made very little noise. I thought she had died on her feet because I didn't know where she was working in the house. Little things like that bothered me, because everything was in slow motion except my mind. Finally, the Lord healed me of this plague. Once I was healed, the Lord led me to go to Guatemala City where Norman Parish prayed for me to be delivered from depression, which was caused by the hepatitis.

A ROCKY CONVERSATION

A few weeks after the hepatitis and my healing, I was again showing movies in the villages, and praying for people to be healed and saved. One night I was showing a Christian film in the coastal town of Omoa. Due to continued weakness from my illness, I almost fell asleep around 10 o'clock when a teenage girl came up from behind and threw rocks at me. I was angry and preached so intensely that a 21 year-old man accepted Jesus Christ as his Savior. He, in turn, preached, and others gave their hearts to the Lord.

THE PROMISE

On Mother's Day, Missionary Daniel Baldwin, flew from Livingston, Guatemala to San Pedro Sula. I had promised Daniel that if he would fly to Honduras I would show him some coastal villages where he could drop gospel tracts. Deany didn't want me to go because of the poor visibility. During this time of the year in May, farmers burned off their corn stubble, which produced ashes and haze. But because of my promise to Daniel, I went. Daniel and I took out the back seat of the 25-year-old Cessna, and in its place put in a barrel, half-filled with gasoline. We landed in La Ceiba to pick up an airplane part, then flew down the coast to the Seco River.

A DENOMINATIONAL DEBATE

While in the air, we dropped tracts on the coastal villages and got into a friendly debate concerning the losing of one's salvation. Daniel was winning the argument because he provided more scriptures than I could muster. As Daniel tried to land the airplane near the turbulent Seco River on this unusually hot day, he had to pull up abruptly because he spotted barbed-wire on the field. Due to a lack of oxygen in the air, the airplane began falling down towards the river.

CALLING ON THE LORD

Before we hit, we both got into one accord and screamed, "JESUS!!!" The Lord rescued us from what would have been certain death. We missed a concrete bridge and an upturned steel rail that could have impaled us, as well as the river that may have carried us out to the sea while flipping us over several times. When we got out of the plane I told Daniel, "See, I told you God was a Calvinist (a believer is secure in God)!!"

THE RESCUERS COME PADDLING

The people in the local village got into their dugout canoes and crossed the river to the wreckage. They thought we were dead, and I'm sure they were going to "relieve us" of all of our valuables - so the thieves would not get them later! Afterwards we were picked up by a Missionary Aviation Fellowship pilot who flew us to Trujillo. From there we took a commercial prop-plane to Tegucigalpa. This trip was memorable because the pilot flew about 100 feet above the mountains the whole way. I offered my vomit bag to the lady sitting to my right. She gladly took it because hers was full. From Tegucigalpa we flew back to San Pedro Sula. But all was not lost on this trip, as I met a wonderful charismatic couple from El Cajon, California. Upon returning home, Deany was very nice to me. She could have said, "I told you not to go!"

MISTER WHO?

One day while I was in town, a 72 year-old Honduran man came to our home to visit me. People had told him that a wise man lived up on the side of the mountain. He had a question to ask this man. He asked Deany, who was home, what this man's name was. She answered, "Brother Ken." He responded, "Brother Quien?" They went back and forth for a while, until she finally explained Ken was my name, not "Brother Who" ("quien" means "who" in Spanish). Finally, when I arrived, he asked me what I thought about him marrying a 17 year-old girl. I told him he wasn't looking for a wife. He was looking for a servant to take care of him in his old age. I added that this was not a good idea at all. I hope he took my advice.

THE SNAKE BITE

One afternoon a 50 year-old Honduran man came to our house for prayer for his swollen, snake-bitten foot, which was wrapped in gauze. We prayed, and he later came back to show us that the swelling had gone down and he was healed. We asked him what kind of snake bit him, and he said it was a Fer-de-Lance. Earlier that month, our boys had run over a Fer-de-Lance on their bicycles at the children's park. The man told us that the Fer-de-Lance was the most dangerous viper in all of Honduras. It is comparable to a cobra.

INSTANCES OF GOD'S PROTECTION

* Jack Morris flipped over our Solex moped on the rocky road in front of our house, and ended up with only a bad cut on his arm.

* James broke his arm on the same Solex when he ran into an uncovered manhole, a mile away from our house. Later, Steve and James were thrown off of Casper, Steve's horse, on their heads, while riding home one evening. They could have been severely hurt, but only sustained minor injuries.

* When we had a water shortage, our boys took their baths in a stream further up the mountain. As Steve was climbing over the barbed-wire fence, he cut his arm and had to have stitches.

* David and I were driving downtown in the Blazer when a car approaching us - the wrong way on a one-way street – hit us on the passenger side where David was sitting. A few moments earlier, David had his arm hanging outside the door and I was impressed to tell him to put it inside. The car hit us exactly where David's arm had been.

* One school break when we were at the coast spear-fishing, Danny speared a scorpion fish on the ocean floor. When he picked up the fish he did not know that the poison in its fins was as bad as a rattlesnake bite. I didn't know it either. All I did was lay hands on him and pray that the swelling would go down. The Lord healed him and the swelling finally went down.

*   Years later when JoAnna had 104 fever in Cuernavaca, Mexico, I was so tired from ministering that all I could do was to put my hand on her feverish body and ask the Lord to heal her. The next morning the fever had left her body.

"It's not by might, nor by power, but by His Spirit."

WE NEEDED MORE CHAIRS

One afternoon as we were driving by the soccer stadium, I saw smoke rising from that area. Then we saw a man carrying six chairs on his back. I asked him how much he wanted for the chairs. He looked at me like I was a "stupid gringo." I didn't know that he had just stolen them from the soccer stadium. A riot had occurred because too many ticket holders to a soccer game had been turned away. This was a common practice in the 1970's - to sell more tickets to a game than there were seats in the stadium.

PAYING OUR BILLS

I have always known that my Heavenly Father is rich, and that I am one of His adopted sons. So in the very beginning I decided to always make it as easy on me, and as difficult as I could on God in terms of finances – because financial obligations didn't seem to bother Him. In 1973 our rent was $105 per month in San Pedro Sula, which we paid one month in advance instead of one month behind. In fact, we did this with all of the bills if we could. At this time, we had just been granted our own television time by Channel 7. We were able to pay for the TV programs one month ahead as we did with our other bills. Not knowing anything about TV programming, we split the hour-long Saturday morning program into two segments, including a 30-minute Christian film and a guest speaker.

The next year we had a 15-minute program on Saturday mornings, and five-minute evening programs on healing, salvation, the family, the Holy Spirit, forgiveness and relationships. The following year we programmed four-minute videos that were produced in El

Paso. Paying for everything in advance made it easy on me. Praise the Lord!

PASTORAL VISITATION

On the evenings when we had no services at the house (and later downtown), Deany and I would visit members of our church family. This visitation proved to be one of our greatest delights. These humble people would gladly welcome us to sit down at the entrance to their homes, while one of their children would run to a nearby, family-owned store to buy a warm, family-sized Pepsi Cola. The entrance to the home was always where visitors were entertained, in these humble family dwellings.

Sometimes we could see our neighbor, Rosa, making her tortillas by hand on the earthen oven outside her house. We don't know if we did Rosa Castro a favor or not by running electricity from our house to hers. Previously, they went to bed when darkness fell. After the Castros received electric lighting they began living like Americans – reading school books and fighting gnats until late in the evening. I hope we did them more good than harm?!

MIRACLES EVERY THURSDAY

From sundown Wednesday until sundown Thursday was my weekly "fast day." I wasn't trying to make the Lord do anything, but I knew this did me a lot of good spiritually. Ordinarily, I would do the work of an evangelist and visit people and hand out tracts. However, Thursdays were different. Mysteriously, people would come to see us on Thursday (I'm sure drawn by the Holy Spirit or prompted by an angel). They would come walking, in personal cars, in taxis, on horseback, on bicycles and motorbikes to our house to visit with me. On Thursdays I got to be a pastor and counselor. I've often wondered what would have happened if I had fasted on more days? I really enjoyed those days of ministry as pastor and counselor.

HOW PEOPLE GET THEIR NAMES

Many babies were named "Fifi" after Hurricane Fifi, which came in September, 1974. When our neighbor, Olimpia, was in labor, I drove her to the hospital very early one morning. Since she and Victor, her husband, were having marital problems, she named the baby Kenny, after her favorite missionary! But when they got back together, she renamed the baby, Victor. When Mrs. Herrera had a baby boy, she named him Dennis after our co-worker, Dennis Key. Celerino Serrano and his wife had a baby girl, and named her Diny after Deany. I was feeling left out until I returned to Honduras and found that our friend, church member and maid, Norma, named her daughter, Kennia. The names of these children were really an honor for all of us working in Mexico and Honduras.

SUMMERTIME '74

In the summer of 1974 we returned to the States so our four sons could go to Lakewood Church's summer camp in North Texas. Deany found jobs for the boys in Houston and in the Texas panhandle. I purchased a 30-day, Greyhound bus pass and traveled through the Midwest and Southeast ministering and buying supplies for the following school year.

That summer I was completely exhausted to the point that I was weary emotionally, physically and even spiritually. One day I called Deany in tears, except for the fact that my body was too dry to produce the water for the tears. As I sat down in a worn-out, stuffed chair in an old hotel near the bus station in Tulsa, Oklahoma, a large, heavy-set man walked into the lobby and handed me a gospel tract, saying, "Bud, this will be good for you." This was the first time in my life anyone had ever handed me a tract. I'll never forget how refreshing that experience was on that particular evening in Tulsa.

MOTORBIKING BACK

Our twins, Daniel and David, saved enough money to buy one motorcycle to take back to Honduras with them. On our way back to Honduras we let the boys ride the motorcycle on the dirt roads behind our Chevrolet Blazer. We always seemed to be the first to leave school, and the last to get back to school, because there was always one more thing to get done. As we drove over these familiar mountain roads back to San Pedro Sula, we were not prepared for the surprise awaiting us on September 17, 1974.

Chapter 4

SAN PEDRO SULA, HONDURAS
(1974-1975)

HURRICANE FIFI AND CRUSADES

Arriving back in San Pedro Sula the second week in September, we found that our watchman, Froelan, a member of our church fellowship, had stolen and then sold some of our belongings. I took Froelan with me to show me where he had sold some of the most important items, so I could buy them back. I bought back my lawnmower, a gospel film and a few other items. I asked his dad why he would steal from us, and his dad said, "That's what you get; you never should have hired him to be a watchman in the first place." However, looking for Froelan and our stolen possessions was a good experience for me because I learned the location of the "red light" district. Later we passed out gospel tracts and witnessed in that colonia. I quickly learned in that district that I needed to keep my eyes open, as well as to hold these young ladies' hands when I prayed for them to accept Christ as their Savior.

A TEST OF FAITH

When we were traveling through Mexico, en route to Honduras, we stopped in Tuxpan, on the Gulf of Mexico and spent the night with Paul Koehler. I felt impressed to give Paul an offering for his ministry. Back in San Pedro Sula I told Deany that I didn't want her to work at the school again, because I needed her to help me with the ministry. We agreed that if $500 came in by Monday, she wouldn't be the school nurse and librarian. That Friday we received a $500 check from the Koehlers in Tuxpan, Mexico, which to us was a miracle. We had brought so many books from the States that we decided to start a Christian library in our home. Now Deany was our librarian as well as the boys' nurse.

ON TOP OF THE MOUNTAIN

On September 17, 1974, Dan and David hiked to the top of the mountain to camp out with a couple of their school friends. It rained all night and they came home the next morning soaking wet with tent and sheets in hand, completely unaware that a "category five" hurricane was brewing off the coast of Honduras. When we asked them why they didn't come home, they replied, "we just wanted to see if we could camp out in the rain." Hurricane Fifi was to inflict one billion dollars worth of property damage in Honduras, killing 6,000 to 10,000 people.

PSALMS 91 TO THE RESCUE

The following morning during devotionals in our home, we read Psalms 91 and asked the Lord for divine protection - as we were feeling the full force of the hurricane. The little creek on the left of our house was now a block-wide, raging river, flowing down from the top of the mountain. On the right of our house a huge tree fell, hitting our fence. Some of the church family moved in with us since their houses were made of tin, wood and cardboard. Our neighbors, Aida, Toni and their family were really fearful during this time.

THE GOOD, THE BAD AND THE UGLY

The "good" thing about the hurricane was that the mail requests for free Christian literature from our ministry's radio and TV programs increased from two letters per week to twelve. Also, missionaries from all different denominations worked together to help the refugees. We were the only missionaries with a 4-wheel drive vehicle, so we were privileged to help others make deliveries of goods to outlying areas.

The "bad" thing that happened after Hurricane Fifi was that the local people became very "picky" about the taste of the canned foods from the United States. The Honduran people did not like sweet foods. They thought the canned pork and beans were too sweet. Also, many of the clothes were too large due to the difference between American and Honduran sizes.

The "ugly" incident involved a colonel in the Honduran Army who stored many of the medicines and canned goods in a warehouse for his own use. When the TV reporters came to investigate, he burned the warehouse to the ground. What a waste of goods, which could have been used to help these homeless refugees.

THE SECRET BEHIND THE STORM

A few months later, Gloria King, a Mennonite missionary from Tegucigalpa, the capital of Honduras, spent the night in our home. She told us what a Spirit-filled Catholic, who had been on the Honduran President's Cabinet, had related to the missionary prayer group prior to the hurricane. Communist China wanted to buy property in Honduras in order to get a foothold in Central America. This cabinet member had resigned his post in protest. I believe three out of the five cabinet members were Communists. The prayer group of missionaries and Hondurans began to fast and pray for 40 days. Shortly after the fast ended, Hurricane Fifi came through Honduras. Because of the extensive damage, China decided not to buy property in Honduras. This allowed the United States to step in and help Honduras financially.

RELIEF FROM BRENHAM

John Crawford and Johnny Martinez, from Brenham, Texas rented an 18-wheeler truck, loaded it with medical supplies, food and clothing, and drove it as far as Mexico City. The truck's trailer was too high, and was crushed under a Mexican bridge. The determined men rented a Mexican trailer, reloaded it and brought it to Honduras. We used these supplies to help the refugees in the camps. Later, we showed gospel movies, trying to reach some of the Cuban medical teams who were also working in the refugee camps.

LAKES, NOT ROADS

One day John Crawford and I loaded 800 pounds of rice on top of our Chevy Blazer, and went to one of the villages to distribute it. As we drove, we came upon a low spot in the road which had literally become a lake. I paid a 12 year-old boy to walk in front of us; as long as he walked, I thought we could drive without drowning out the car engine. If the little boy were to start swimming, then I would have to back up. Praise the Lord, we made it all the way across this newly formed lake, and delivered the rice.

LEARNING FINANCIAL ACCOUNTABILITY

Seven thousand dollars came in to our ministry, Christian Witness Crusade, for hurricane relief purposes. At this time our TV ministry was coming along pretty well, and I was tempted to use $1,000 of the relief money for a reel-to-reel video projector. The temptation persisted, as an American entrepreneur convinced me of my need to produce my own TV programs in Honduras. I bought the projector and used it as much as we could. But I was sorry afterwards that all this money did not go into the hurricane relief fund as it was intended. Today, this would be called the misappropriation of funds. This experience helped me learn that good, Christian stewards, being unprepared to manage a sudden increase in finances, is very dangerous! (My heart goes out to people who have a sudden influx of financial wealth - without having learned accountability).

NEIGHBORHOOD DANGERS

After the flood, James and some other neighbor boys were in a nearby swimming hole. A man came by with some rocks and threatened to hurt them if they did not give him their watches. They did!

Later, our son David was pushing his dirt bike along a mountain trail on private property. A watchman with a rifle, who was guarding a house on this property, stopped David and confiscated his bike. He then demanded that David give him $10 or he'd lose his bike. David came home and borrowed $10 and then went back and got his bike.

COMMUNICATION PROBLEMS

Dan and David, twins, worked in the summer saving their money to buy a dirt bike. They were supposed to take turns riding it. One day they began wrestling in the street over whose turn it was to have the dirt bike. I called from the stairs, "Let him have it." David shouted back, "I will, as soon as I get my hand free!" We were obviously talking about different things. (This is called communication, right?) Another time a mouse was running across the road in Boerne, Texas, and I told Steve to get it (meaning, stomp it). He picked up the mouse by the tail and it bit him on the hand. Again, we have great communication in our family!

GOING BACK ON THE AIR

While we were waiting for the TV station to re-open after the hurricane, John Crawford and I went to the Central American radio station to inquire about radio time. Soon we were on the radio 30 minutes a day, seven days a week. Not long afterwards, column space in La Prensa and El Tiempo, the San Pedro Sula newspapers, was also donated to us.

Dr. Tito Handel, an Arab dentist, whose newscast preceded our TV program, "Jesus Cristo Vive Hoy" (Jesus Christ Lives Today), once told me, "Your Spanish accent is very thick, but I listen to your program all the time because I understand your heart." I felt better after he finished the whole sentence because I knew my accent was thick.

MONKEYS, ALLIGATORS AND A CANOE FULL OF PEOPLE

One Saturday afternoon, while the Crawfords from Brenham were still visiting us, we decided to go canoeing down a huge river that flows through a nearby jungle. Having boarded the canoe, we sat only two inches above the waterline. I told everybody to be very still as we motored down the river. Soon we saw 40-pound black monkeys on the right bank, and 20-pound black monkeys with white faces on the left bank. We stopped by the shore to watch the monkeys. Suddenly we began hearing a reptile under the water sucking in air for three to four minutes, warning us to move away. To this day I don't know if it was a large python, or a huge cayman (alligator). We backed away very slowly and very cautiously and never returned. As I relate this story, the hair on the back of my neck still bristles.

BURNIE DAVIS CRUSADES

After the "hurricane refugees" were taken out of the army tents, concrete block homes were built for them. It was at this time that John Osteen and Lakewood Church of Houston financed a crusade with Evangelist Burnie Davis in San Pedro Sula and later in Tegucigalpa. Thousands of people responded to Christ in both cities through healings, deliverances from evil spirits, salvation and the baptism in the Holy Spirit.

SMALLER CRUSADES

After the Burnie Davis Crusade in Campo Marathon, other Christian brothers came from the States to help us in smaller crusades. These evangelists included J.D. Spann (Houston), Bill Smith (Tulsa), John and Vernon Harris (Nashville, South Carolina), Jerry Norman (Jamaica, New York), Jerry Grey (Los Angeles), Harold Walker (Pine Mountain Valley, Georgia), Jack Morris (Beaumont, Texas), Dennis Key (Houston) and George Pike (Bethlehem, Georgia). These crusades brought salvation, deliverance, the baptism in the Holy Spirit and healing to many in San Pedro Sula and surrounding towns.

COMPETITION AMONG THE BRETHREN

However, as the Lord worked, so did the enemy in conjunction with these campaigns. Because of the intensity of the attacks, I needed help in some emotional areas myself. The Lord sent Jack Enders, from Austin, Texas, to help put me back together both emotionally and spiritually. Due to a "power play" among some of the missionaries and evangelists, I was squeezed out of participating in the second crusade in Tegucigalpa. This happened as a result of differences in doctrine regarding water baptism. The differences centered around using the name Jesus Christ as opposed to the titles Father, Son and Holy Spirit when administering water baptism.

JACK ENDERS

Jack Enders was the brother who prayed for me and encouraged me during this difficult time. We all need a friend like Jack, who personally encourages and helps place us back into the body of Christ. Praise the Lord!

A LONG OVERDUE REVELATION

Twenty years later, the Lord woke me up in Houston early one morning and put the baptismal formula together for me, saying, "This works: In the authority of God the Father, and by the power of the Holy Spirit, I baptize you into the body of Jesus Christ. Amen." I had always been a seeker of scriptural truth, which sometimes caused me to be misunderstood by some of my orthodox, evangelical brethren. Rejection always hurts, but the Lord uses it to keep us in a place of humility.

THE STOLEN MOTORBIKE

One Sunday afternoon while we were all upstairs in the house watching our black and white TV, someone stole the twins' motorbike. The thief came in through the outside gate and pushed the motorbike down the road before starting it. We reported the crime to the police. Several months later they came to the house looking for us, saying that the bike was at the police station. One officer asked if we were the ones who had lost a motorbike. The bike was in three cement bags with its frame. Dan and David were very disappointed, but began to rebuild the bike piece by piece. They flipped a coin to see who would "get" to go to Guatemala City to purchase motorcycle parts that were unavailable in Honduras. Three days later David came home, sunburned and tired. He was out of money, and had to hitchhike back with the motorcycle parts. This was a hard experience for a high school student. But the boys worked hard and rebuilt the motorbike. The discipline from the experience served them well. David later became an engineer in Ft. Worth, and Dan the owner of a construction company in Houston.

GROWING A FAMILY CHURCH

We received a letter from a viewer of our TV program, requesting prayer for Juana, who had been hit by a car. We went to Colonia Cabanas at Pasaje San Cristobal and met Juana's family. After prayer, we met Lesly Herrera, Juana's 12 year-old cousin, who had impetigo, an infectious skin disease, on her face. We prayed for Lesly and came back a week later for another meeting to find Lesly's face completely healed. This was the beginning of a weekly backyard meeting at the Herrera home.

Months later, an American evangelist and I were distributing gospel tracts at one of the local high schools, where we met Miriam Salinas, a school teacher. Miriam asked us if we would visit her mother, who enjoyed our TV program. After visiting Mrs. Guadalupe Salinas, and praying for her to receive Christ as her Savior, we started our second series of backyard services. While more youth attended the Herrera meetings than adults, the opposite was true at the meetings in the Salinas' back yard.

As the church fellowships grew, Doris Padilla offered to give us some land in Colonia Sanceri. Kiki Panting, a Honduran of English and Italian heritage, helped me with the TV programs. He suggested writing Frank Sinatra to ask him for the needed $5,000 to start building a simple framed church building. (Kiki explained that Mr.

Sinatra gave donations to various church groups). Somehow, since we were called to disciple young Christians, the Lord never allowed us to construct church buildings.

A NEW EXPERIENCE

One morning, Carlos Prado brought his mistress, Sandra, over to meet me. Carlos had recently been saved, baptized in water and filled with the Holy Spirit. After his conversion, we had talked about the right thing to do with Sandra and their five year-old daughter. Sandra didn't like the counsel I had previously given Carlos, so she put a butcher knife in her purse. Carlos told me she was going to kill me. I was all dressed up to go to the TV station to do my daily program. After we had a brief prayer (with my eyes open), I asked Deany to serve them lemonade. I would return in an hour from Channel Seven's TV station.

KIKI PANTING

When I returned I brought Kiki Panting with me. As soon as Sandra saw Kiki, she screamed and he ran upstairs to our living room. (Kiki had "dated" Sandra before he was saved in the crusade). We ministered deliverance to Sandra, and she accepted the Lord as her Savior. Because of greed in my heart, I suggested that Sandra join the local Mennonite church, and that Carlos and his family keep coming to our church (because Carlos had a job and was giving tithes). Sandra was later married and is still serving the Lord. Kiki continued to help me in the TV ministry, and was faithful to Blanca, his wife, the rest of their married lives.

CARLOS AND IRMA

Carlos and Irma Prado have since returned to Bolivia, where he holds tent meetings all over the country. In one report, the blind eyes of six people were opened, and several deaf people received their hearing.

MANY FRIENDS AND GREAT TRIPS

I shall always be grateful for friends like Harold Walker, George Lowery, Joseph Reyes, Jack Morris, Ray Wallace, Don James, Paul Rau, Warren Crane, my wife and five children and perhaps 70 others who have traveled with me to Spain, Mexico, Central America and Belize.

SUMMER OF '75

As we left Honduras, driving back to Texas through Mexico, I let the boys take turns driving while sitting in the seat with me. If they hit the white lines on either side of the road it was time for the next son to drive. This is how we passed five days on the road from Honduras to Texas. That summer we went to Alex Blomerth's TV station in El Paso, Texas and filmed our five-minute TV programs. We took these videos back to Channel 7 in San Pedro Sula to be viewed all over Honduras. Deany and I found jobs for our four sons. Steve, after selling his horse and working, saved enough money to get a motorcycle. David and Dan each had their own motorcycles (dirt bikes) by this time after working that summer.

GOOD SAMARITAN

Traveling back to Honduras in early September, we were pulling a small pop-up trailer and carrying two motorcycles. Without pulling over onto the shoulder, Deany and I attempted to switch drivers. As a result of that youthful foolishmess, the small trailer flipped upside down. A Spirit-filled Catholic priest stopped to help us turn the trailer back over on its tires again. We then followed him to Saltillo, near Monterrey, Mexico, where he got us a motel room and dinner.

A CHECK-POINT BORDER SURPRISE

When we entered Honduras from Guatemala, we were surprised when the Honduran border people abruptly demanded $600.00 for the taxes on our Chevy Blazer (or it would be impounded at the border). Thankfully, we acknowledged the $600.00 that Newman Peyton, Jr. had given us before leaving Texas for Honduras.

BACK IN SAN PEDRO SULA

The next day we traveled towards Honduras, traveling through heavy fog. Because the headlights were doing no good in the fog, our sons took turns holding a flashlight out of the passenger window so I could see the road, and avoid a wrong turn which would have sent us over a 1,500 foot cliff. Three days later we arrived in San Pedro Sula in time to put the boys in school, and for us to pastor the local church again.

As we drove over the familiar mountainous terrain we couldn't help but wonder what our third year would be like in Honduras. Our first year was hepatitis and an airplane crash. Our second year was the Hurricane Fifi disaster. During our third missionary year, little did we know what an earthquake could do to Central America - but we were soon to find out!

Chapter 5

SAN PEDRO SULA HONDURAS
(1975-1976)

CHURCH ACTIVITIES AND EARTHQUAKES

Floyd and Beth Alves, who are now involved with Intercessors International, drove down to Honduras with us and spent some time ministering in several of the local churches. At this point we moved the church facilities from under our house on the side of the mountain to the second floor of a downtown building. We also had two cell groups which continued to meet at the homes of Lesly Herrera and Mrs. Guadalupe Salinas. The last Saturday night of each month, the church fellowship ate together, and I let the young people take turns sharing lessons that I had taught earlier.

REPETITION WORKS

There were signs that our young people needed repetitious Bible training. During our youth meetings, sometimes Tomas, one of our young men, would write on the blackboard 1 Chronicles instead of 1 Corinthians. This exercise helped me to realize that what we take for granted needed more "drilling", and I was able to monitor how much our young people were actually learning. We also had communion and water baptism during these once-a-month services. Sometimes we even had a foot washing service.

MAKING LEADERS

The ministry was taking shape as the Lord was producing leaders from among the congregation, such as Mark Werner, Kiki Panting, Omar and Connie Rodriguez, Lesly Herrera, Carlos Prado, Tona Betencourth and Guadalupe Salinas. The two home meetings, on Thursday and Friday nights, were really yard meetings when it was not raining.

DENNIS AND PAULA KEY

Dennis and Paula Key and two children, from Houston, came down to help us in our ministry. Dennis and Paula graciously gave of themselves in helping us in San Pedro Sula, with construction on the downtown church building, mechanical work on cars and teaching the people. Later they ministered in Guatemala, before moving back to Houston.

JACK AND PEGGIE MORRIS

Jack and Peggie Morris, from the One Way Inn Church in Beaumont, Texas flew down to San Pedro Sula and helped to cover our kitchen floor with linoleum. Jack shared with me the teaching they were doing in Beaumont. This mainly consisted of Hebrews 6:1-2, which says:

> "Therefore, leaving the principles of the doctrine of Christ, let us go on unto perfection; not laying again the foundation of repentance from dead works, and of faith toward God, of the doctrine of baptisms, and of laying on of hands, and of resurrection of the dead, and of eternal judgment. And this will we do, if God permit."

Jack showed me the value of teaching on these six basic principles to a young church fellowship. During the third year in Honduras, we taught Hebrews 6:1-2 practically every night, with the exception of Monday - which was our personal family time.

JOHN AND BETTY CRAWFORD

John Crawford, from Brenham, Texas brought us a blue school bus that we used to minister to the people in the banana plantations each week. I would let our church people go with me on the bus, provided they distributed tracts and witnessed in the villages to the lost people. These trips served as a wonderful opportunity for me to disciple our people in witnessing to others.

THE EARTH MOVED

In January of 1976, Guatemala was hit by a devastating earthquake that killed as many as 25,000 people. The epicenter of the earthquake was only 75 miles from our house in San Pedro Sula. At 4:00 o'clock in the morning our huge bookcase fell to the floor, and three of our boys came running out of their rooms. Steve slept through the whole episode. Dogs were howling; roosters were crowing; donkeys were braying and people were running everywhere as fires broke out all over the city.

AFTER EFFECTS

The next day we saw twisted buildings, broken gas lines and fallen electric wires. Even though we felt the tremors at our home, the major damage was done in Guatemala City, Guatemala. Many people in Guatemala City died as a result of suffocation and later from lung diseases, caused by dust from the mud bricks. It was now our turn to help the Christian churches in Guatemala care for Guatemalans. They had helped us following Hurricane Fifi in 1974. We responded by taking clothes, blankets, medicines and financial aid to the victims of this earthquake.

CONCRETE COMMUNITIES

After the earthquake, Norman Parrish and other missionaries and ministers in Guatemala oversaw the building of thousands of concrete block houses in the colonias (suburbs) around Guatemala

City. Norman handled thousands of dollars that poured in from all over the world to help give these displaced peoples a place to live in their new communities.

GETTING BUSIER

Back in Honduras, this was to be the busiest year of my life. On Monday nights we had family time with the boys. Wednesday night we showed movies in villages. Thursday and Friday nights we had home (cell) meetings. Tuesday and Saturday nights, and Sunday morning and Sunday nights we had church meetings downtown (formerly under our house). Saturday mornings we had family devotionals with our children, before they hurried off to play with their buddies. Meanwhile, I was still doing TV programs five days a week, and radio programs seven days a week. I was now writing for two newspapers, El Tiempo and La Prensa.

SHARING MY PRAYER TIME

In order to keep me going, I had a little place to pray after lunch each day. This was originally built for the maid's quarters. I cleaned this spot and, except for the extreme heat, it was a good place for prayer and meditation. There was a huge, grey scorpion under the wood plank on the floor, and a big, brown tarantula in the corner of the ceiling. I made a pact with them: if they wouldn't bother me, I wouldn't kill them. This truce worked fine with the three of us. These periods of meditation kept me sane, and possibly saved me from a nervous breakdown.

MORNING SICKNESS STRIKES AGAIN

In the meantime (January '76), Deany and I found ourselves with some extra money. I had purchased an airplane ticket in order to attend John Osteen's annual missions conference at Lakewood Church in Houston. But a high ranking government official must have needed my seat on Sahsa Airlines more than I did; I was bumped from my seat and my ticket was cancelled! Feeling a little discouraged, Deany and I decided to go out and celebrate. We checked into the Hotel Bolivar for the night, and ate a huge lobster dinner. Six weeks later, Deany was surprised when morning sickness struck again!

When James, our youngest son, was 10 years old, Deany and I were thinking about adopting twin Honduran baby girls. When Deany realized we were going to have our own child (number five), she quickly shifted gears and found a Mennonite couple near Tegucigalpa who wanted to adopt these twins. The couple had already adopted a boy. Each one of our children responded differently to mother's surprise: Daniel said, "Wow". David said, "Don't you know how to prevent that?" Steven blushed and smiled. James said, "I'm going to be an uncle!" I got a chuckle out of Deany when I came home with a green-painted, hand-made high chair that I bought from a street vendor in downtown San Pedro Sula.

A WOLF IN SHEEP'S CLOTHING

One spring afternoon, our neighbors, Toni and Aida Miranda, introduced us to Samuel, a man from Costa Rica. He delighted us with his version of the "Choo-Choo Train" on his accordion. Samuel told me that $100 had been stolen from him on the bus. That evening at our church service we took an offering, and gave Samuel $100. Shortly thereafter, when he proposed marriage to one of the Salinas' daughters, we thought we'd better investigate who he really was. Samuel told us that his wife and two children had been killed in an automobile accident in San Jose. But when a Mennonite missionary in San José telephoned us and said that Samuel had a living wife and children, we realized that he had been lying to us all along. Praise the Lord for this cooperation among the missionaries! After we confronted Samuel with our discovery, he quickly disappeared. That was $100 worth of experience for me and our church family.

THE HONDURAN FBI

During one evening service in our downtown building, a man with a "hard" face came into our meeting. The Holy Spirit changed my message to "The Love of God." Slowly the hard lines on his face became softer, as the Lord ministered to him. He was investigating all foreigners who might be involved in a car theft ring. After the service, he cordially invited me to meet with him downtown the next day. The other agent asked me what kind of church we were. I told him it was a non-denominational, charismatic Christian church. He asked me what my opinions were about other groups, such as Mormons, Jehovah's Witnesses, etc. My response was that every religious group has a tendency to cut down on crime (not knowing he was a Mormon himself). He liked my answer, and that was the last I saw of these Honduran "FBI" agents. I learned a lesson about speaking something good, if at all possible, regarding any group.

MARK WERNER

Mark Werner, who also worked with Kiki and me with the TV ministry, graduated with law degrees in Honduras and the States. Mark is now practicing law in San Pedro Sula. He and Norma and their five children are pillars in their local church.

OMAR AND CONNIE RODRIGUEZ

Omar and Connie Rodriguez carried on the ministry of our church fellowship. Then Dennis and Paula Key stayed for several months after Deany and I left Honduras to return to the States. The fellowship gradually changed to a more youth-oriented ministry. Later, Omar worked with the Philadelphia and Foursquare Churches. He has ministered in Puerto Rico and Miami, Florida as a teacher/ evangelist. Now Omar has a church and radio station in La Ceiba, Honduras. The attendance is approximately 900 people every Sunday.

EMALENA MUNSON

Emalena Munson, our first adult convert, became a member of the Women's Aglow Fellowship in Honduras. Later she became one of the leaders in this Christian fellowship, and has led many ladies to the Lord.

LESLY HERRERA

Lesly Herrera, our first TV convert, who was healed and saved, was responsible for opening her mother's backyard for home Bible studies where many young people came to know the Lord. She later married Mark Sullivan, an American missionary to Honduras. This couple and their two sons now live and minister in Everett, Washington.

GUADALUPE SALINAS

Guadalupe Salinas and her 11 children now live in Honduras, Florida and New Orleans, Louisiana. We had meetings in her back-yard every Thursday evening, near the downtown area of San Pedro Sula. Many of her Arab and Spanish neighbors came to know the Lord as their Savior. Most of the family now live in Louisiana. Deany and I try to visit them in New Orleans once a year and have services in their home.

TONA BETENCOURTH

Tona Betencourth and Rigoberto, a former alcoholic whom she lived with, finally got married just before his death. Tona, along with Omar and Connie Rodriguez, was very faithful in helping arrange the chairs for the services each evening. She also helped in cleaning the auditorium after the meetings.

BOB AND CAROL CLARK

Bob and Carol Clark, American science and English teachers at the school our children attended in San Pedro Sula, were a great encouragement to our family. Bob helped me many times by watching the generator while I was projecting movies out in the rural villages. Bob strongly disliked Carlos Prado's loud rock music, which blared from his egg delivery trucks. After Carlos' conversion to Christ, the music changed to worship and praise. Previously, Bob wanted to throw a rock at the trucks, but he thoroughly enjoyed the new music. On the other hand, Ruby Rhinehart, a charismatic Catholic leader, thought the praise music was sacrilegious. (You can't please everybody! Ha!). Bob and Carol now live in Malaysia, teaching in a Christian school. Their daughter and son are a nurse and doctor, respectively, in the States.

ROSA CASTRO

Rosa Castro and her family were our next-door neighbors. Two of Rosa's daughters, Rita and Norma, helped Deany do the washing, cooking and house cleaning in order for Deany to be able to do office work and be a full-time mother. The youngest daughter, Maria, had a little cat that enjoyed coming into our house. The cat would watch our two parrots in their cage all day long - wanting to "fellowship" with them, I'm sure!

GETTING CAUGHT

Early one morning before the boys left for school, I found Maria's cat on our dining room table eating my breakfast. I took the cat outside the kitchen door and threw it as far up into the air as I could, with a bit of personal, fleshly satisfaction in my heart. But as I looked over the fence, there was Maria. My triumph turned to sadness, realizing I had hurt Maria. I apologized profusely for the hurt I had caused her. However the cat landed on all fours and escaped unharmed.

DIFFERENT STANDARDS

I have learned that in many of the third world countries, a pet is the only possession some children have that truly belongs to them. While, by contrast, in the United States we have so much. At Christmas I would be personally grieved when the neighbors wanted to see what we gave our children, knowing how little they had. By my country's standards I would not be considered a wealthy man. However, as an American missionary living in a third world country, I was considered very wealthy.

MATURE UNDERSTANDING

Maria now has two children of her own, but she is a single mother. Ordinarily, Christians would judge Maria harshly since she was never married, but the children are her only real possessions. I have a little more insight now as a 62 year-old dad and grandad than I did when I was 38, living in Honduras as an over-worked missionary with four children and a lot of responsibilities.

ERNA MORAN

The last member of our fellowship I'd like to mention is Erna Moran, whom we met at the Catholic Charismatic Center in San Pedro Sula. Erna had married an American and moved from the States to Honduras to work with her husband in the lumber industry. When I met Erna, she was depressed because her husband had left her for a young Honduran woman. She now had the responsibility of raising her two sons and daughter by herself. We would drive the bus by Erna's house and talk her into going with us into the banana plantations to show Christian movies. Gradually the depression subsided, and Erna became a productive part of our church's ministry. Her three children are now grown and doing very well in Honduras.

ANOTHER SUMMER TRIP

As we began to turn the church over to the young men of our fellowship, we started getting ready to return to Texas for the summer. We had given each person in the church a job to do for the next three months.

MORE TV PRODUCTION

In May of 1976, we left our Blazer in San Pedro Sula and flew from Honduras to New Orleans, then caught a bus to Houston. We borrowed Deany's parents' car, and drove to El Paso. While there, we produced 90 five-minute videos in Alex Blomerth's TV station. This time Vic Richards worked with me in producing the videos. We found summer jobs again for the boys, and I made my preaching rounds while Deany helped our four sons. Toward the end of the summer we were planning to fly back to Honduras. Because Deany was seven months pregnant with JoAnna, she had to have a medical release from the doctor saying she was able to travel by air. We were staying at a Lakewood Church cottage in Houston.

OUR PERSONAL EARTHQUAKE

Deany's doctor in Conroe, north of Houston, immediately put her in the hospital because of phlebitis (blood clotting of the leg). He said if the blood clot got loose and went to her heart, she could die. This changed our plans drastically, and we asked our dear friends, Dennis and Paula Key, to look after the church in Honduras for us. After two weeks in the hospital and six weeks of living with our friends Earl and Sue Taft, we were able to move back into our house in Houston. I put the boys in school and encouraged Deany all I could. Even though I missed the ministry tremendously, I could only think of what we could do for our wife and mother at this time.

THE CHANGING OF THE GUARD

The Keys, who later had to leave Honduras, turned the work over to the Cunninghams, another missionary couple. At this time, Omar and Connie Rodriguez began to come forth with their ministry in the church. We lost the older people, but Omar began to draw in other young people and the church began to go a different direction. When the Cunninghams left Honduras, Omar and Connie had stabilized this young church. For this labor of love on the part of Omar and Connie Rodriguez, we are very grateful. Later, Omar worked with the Philadelphia and Foursquare churches. Also, Deany and I learned that God is in charge, not us. He turned the work over to Hondurans even when we, as American missionaries, did not know how or when to make this change.

After rearing four sons we were going to learn what it would be like to have a baby girl grow up in our home in Houston, Texas.

Chapter 6

HOUSTON, TEXAS, 1976-1977

COMING HOME AND NEW BEGINNINGS

After moving back into our house at 1206 Springrock, I painted our baby's room pink. Everybody in the neighborhood thought I was a little too bold in painting the room pink in light of the fact that we had four boys.

IT'S A GIRL!

On October 7, 1976, JoAnna Ruth was born into the Lowry family, weighing in at six pounds, fourteen ounces. By this time the boys and I had made new bedrooms in the attic and garage to go along with our existing three bedrooms. The living room also became a portable bedroom because of our sleeper sofa.

BOREDOM IS HELL

Having had an active ministry in Honduras, I was now bored "spitless" with no ministry in Houston. Brother George Lupo let me preach on his "Old Time Religion Hour" TV program in Spanish. I then found a Mexican Baptist brother washing cars. After telling him that I used to pastor a Baptist church near Houston, he invited me to his cousin's house where I began to hold services three times a week. The family soon realized that I wasn't the kind of Baptist they were, since I raised my hands when I prayed, and clapped my hands when I sang. Since the Baptists were Hispanic, they were too nice to tell me not to return for future services.

A CONVERT IN HOUSTON

Socorro Serrano was the only Catholic in her family, while all the other Serranos were Baptists. After a few months she accepted Jesus as her Savior, and received the baptism in the Holy Spirit. Later, her husband, Juan, and cousin, Jésus, also received the baptism in the Holy Spirit. By this time the Serranos had come to really like me, and we started a church in their home. In the meantime, I was going back and forth to Honduras to see if the Lord still had a place for me in San Pedro Sula. By the way, the Serranos, the Cantús, the Chavez family, the Molanos, the Monterosas and others are still going on with the Lord. Pastor Manuel Montez is now pastoring these Christians along with many others in West Houston. This is truly an international church, with people from Mexico, Central America, South America, Spain and Texas. Pastor Hugo Zelaya, who took my place as pastor, is now in Costa Rica. (Pastor Manuel Montaz became pastor when Reverend Zelaya returned to pastor his former congregation in Costa Rica).

REJECTION HURTS AGAIN

After ministering in various churches on a trip to Honduras, I encountered one of my missionary friends, Nona Jo Alvarado. She said that the other missionaries did not want me to return to San Pedro Sula, because they all thought I was a "oneness" missionary. In theological circles, one is either classified as a trinitarian or a oneness; you believed that God was three in one, or one in three. I never have worked this out too well in my own theology.

In the three years since we left Honduras, God had made many changes in our ministry in San Pedro Sula. Omar Rodriguez was on his way to doing more as a Honduran minister than I could ever have done as an American missionary. It seems that the Lord uses outsiders to begin a ministry, but uses the nationals to establish it.

After I left San Pedro Sula, I stopped over in Guatemala City, feeling sorry for myself. As I told another missionary what had happened, he, too, felt sorry for me. Misery loves company! But as I was walking down the street, the Holy Spirit spoke to me and said, "If you are persecuted for righteousness sake, you are to rejoice and be exceedingly glad, for great is your reward in heaven". I immediately repented, and literally raised my hands on the street corner and praised the Lord. Rejoicing in the Lord is the perfect medicine for self-pity.

LOSE SOME, GAIN SOME

In 1977 I tried to obtain TV time in Guatemala, Salvador, Honduras, Nicaragua, Costa Rica and Panama. However, since I was not living in Central America, this TV ministry never came to pass. From 1978 to 1997 I have been ministering with other brothers in 28 countries: Jamaica, Canada, Mexico, England, Europe, the Philippines, China, Russia and Africa. I thought my ministry was put on hold when I came out of Honduras, but I am so grateful that the Lord has opened so many new doors of ministry to us.

THE VALUE OF PRAYING IN TONGUES

In 1988, Sidney Fontenot from Sulphur, Louisiana and I held a crusade with Pastor Rojas in Miramar, Puntarenas, Costa Rica, where we saw many people come to the Lord. One evening as we were returning to the pastor's house, I saw a huge, brown tarantula slowly crossing our path. I gently put my shoe on top of it until somebody could bring a jar. I wanted to take the tarantula home and show it to my grandchildren. When they arrived with the jar, the tarantula was gone. Knowing now that it had crawled up my trouser leg, I began a very energetic dance. Finally when it fell out, I was more relieved than the tarantula was when we put it in the jar.

While Sidney stayed in Miramar, Puntarenas to finish the crusade, I went with Evangelist Artavia to preach in one of his church fellowships up in the mountains where it was cold and damp. That night before I preached I was really shivering. I decided to pray in tongues as loud as I could to see how much good it would do my body. After two hours of praying in the Spirit, I began to feel warm all over. That night we prayed for everyone's physical healing and salvation. To this day, I'll never forget the value of praying in the Spirit for my whole being: body, soul and spirit. Amen! Besides the good I received from praying in the Spirit (Jude 20), others received healing, deliverance, salvation and the baptism in the Holy Spirit.

GREED, MAN'S PROVISION

I never looked upon myself as being a greedy person. A deacon in the Lesley Baptist Church once called me "ambitious," but I had never been called greedy. After selling my Volkswagon camper, I used the money to buy two Volkswagon "beetles." Brother Richard McCall, who sold the cars to me, became offended because he thought I tried to sell the cars for too much money. From that experience I learned that greed was just as much a part of my flesh as it was in any local car salesman's. It didn't take too long for me to get out of the car business, and concentrate full-time on missionary work and living by faith. (By the way, I'm not as hard on car salesmen due to this experience).

GOD'S INSTRUCTION ABOUT PROVISIONS

One night in Lawton, OK., Billy Paul Daniels and I spent the night in the Thompson's home. During the night I thought about writing 100 of my charismatic friends to send me $1.00 each month to help support our missionary travels (postcards were only 3 cents each and I could help the Lord to support us with $97.00 each month). Early the next morning, He spoke this to me: "How would you like for your children to go around in the neighborhood asking your neighbors to supply food for your breakfast?" I told the Lord that this would really embarrass me. He replied, "You would really embarrass Me if you looked to anyone besides ME for your support." I have never forgotten this conversation with the Lord, and I hope I never will. (He uses people to provide funds for missionaries, but instead of looking to people, we are to look to Him alone).

A VISIT TO HONDURANS IN THE U.S.A.

One last note before ending our missionary trips to Latin America: Wallace Curlee and I stopped to minister in Kenner, La., with the Salinas family who had moved from Honduras. Later, George Lowery (no kin) and I would minister to this terrific family. There are many Central Americans now living in the New Orleans area who are helping the city to recover from Hurricane Katrina.

GRACE AND MERCY: GOD'S PROVISIONS

From 1967 to 1997 my Heavenly Father has been demonstrating to me and my family His grace and mercy in all of His provisions to us. Please bear with me as I list some of these blessed events from the Throne of God:

1) In 1967, A neighbor in West Houston helped Deany find our present home.

2) My former church family in Waller, Texas provided the down-payment for our house. The house mortgage was paid in full in July of 1996.

3) Friends in Odessa, Texas gave our four sons their first rods and reels.

4) Friends in Powder Springs, Georgia gave our four sons their first Huffy bicycles.

5) A family tent was given by a friend in Montgomery, Alabama.

6) A Chevy Blazer and Shasta trailer were given to us by a friend in San Antonio.

7) A set of new clothes and cowboy boots were given to each of our boys by friends in San Antonio.

8) A school bus was given by friends in Brenham, Texas.

9) Another school bus and a new set of tires were given by friends in Hereford, Texas.

10) Friends in San Pedro Sula, Honduras funded a 30-day mission trip to Europe.

11) God has always made it possible for either my wife or another minister to travel with me throughout the world.

12) Margaret Weyrauch in Marfa, Texas sent me money in the mail for exactly the amount I had pledged to a missionary in Monterrey, Mexico.

13) The Lord has even given us incidental things, like a set of big-headed, wooden golf clubs from Sandy Spring, Georgia. (By the way, I am not a very good golfer).

14) The Lord sent me a phone card from McAlester, Oklahoma.

15) A lady in a senior citizens home in Houston lent me her credit card to pay for a motel in Matehuala, Mexico.

16) The Lord provided a TV station and producers for us in El Paso, Texas to make TV programs for Honduras.

17) The Lord sent us the money for our first refrigerator in Honduras, from Golden, Colorado.

18) The Lord provided funds from Aurora, Colorado for our ministry trip to Jamaica.

19) Strangers in Temixco, Morelos, Mexico invited us to their home to rest and take a bath.

20) Friends in Sugarland, Texas paid for a much-needed surgery for Deany after JoAnna was born.

21) A missionary friend in Jamaica, New York helped Steve buy a horse in Honduras.

22) Friends from Nashville, South Carolina fixed the motor on my Datsun car.

23) A dentist in west Houston put braces on three of my children's teeth.

24) Plumbers and electricians in our local church in west Houston have worked on our house for no pay.

25) Friends and relatives in Lufkin, Fulshear, Hockley, Gilchrist, Spring, Ft. Worth, San Antonio, Dallas, Beaumont and Brenham, Texas, as well as Houston, have blessed us in our overseas ministries.

26) God has provided us with homes to stay in all over the US, Canada, Mexico, Central America, Jamaica, Europe, Africa, Asia, Russia, etc.

27) Besides a house, two buses, two trailers, one pick-up and one step van, He has provided us with over a half a dozen cars, vans and stationwagons! WOW! P.T.L.

28) This list could go on and on. God has blessed us more than we could ever have done on our own – even if Deany, our five children and I had each, individually worked over 80 hours per week. Striving to be obedient children brings His provisions of grace and mercy more than we could ever begin to tell.

Please know that Deany and I have almost never sought material wealth. However, we have prayed for wisdom, knowledge and understanding due to our needs in this ministry as missionaries. But as a side product, God has blessed us through His grace and mercy by meeting all of our needs and keeping us healthy. Thank You, Jesus! Hallelujah!!

MINISTRY DOORS

Jesus says that He is the only door to the Father. We, too, as God's children, are smaller doors to different places in the world. For example, a minister in Pine Mountain Valley, Georgia opened the door for me to minister in the Philippines. A pastor in Wahalla, South Carolina opened a door for me in China. An editor in Groveton, Texas invited me to minister among Pentecostals in East Texas. An evangelist in Mobile, Alabama took me with him to Russia. Ministry friends Dale Hussey and Don Dessurault, in Ontario, Canada presented me to the North American Indians. The above could also be said concerning the many doors that have opened into Mexico, Central America and Jamaica. Finally, a publisher/minister friend has opened the present door to hold crusades and pastors' seminars in East Africa (See below).

FAMILY UPDATE 1997

I am still traveling and ministering, both in the US and overseas. At present, we are planning to be in Kenya, East Africa, from August 6-26, 1997, with Brother Michael Simati, holding five crusades and two pastors' seminars. Also, we are to hold crusades and seminars in Puebla and Morelos, Mexico, in the second half of November, 1997. Deany, my faithful, wonderful wife, is helping to care for her 92 year-old dad in Hereford, Texas, as well as practicing midwifery in Houston (since 1982). She just completed her 300th birth this year.

At present, Daniel and Kelly Lowry of Houston, and their five children, are ministering back and forth in Central America, helping in particular Darrell and JoAnn Stratton in Conilla, Quiche, Guatemala.

David and Donna Lowry and their two sons live in Fort Worth, Texas, where he works as an engineer. David is trying to become a full-time engineering consultant so he can travel with me overseas, even to East Africa this summer, if possible.

Steven and Cindy Lowry and two children live in Virginia Beach, Virginia where he works as a civil engineer. Steve is a strong supporter of Christian Witness Crusade, and does home Bible studies.

James and Jennifer Lowry and two children live in Houston. James is a medical salesman for Johnson and Johnson, and works along with Jennifer in their local church with the young people.

JoAnna Lowry, a college sophomore, is presently back home, working to pay off school loans. This will enable her to return to college in the fall of 1997.

It is my prayer that all of our children and grandchildren will be involved in the Lord's work either in the US or overseas as missionaries.

Here's a story told to me recently by my doctor brother, Gene Lowry, who, as a colonel in the Air Force, was stationed in Japan in 1976: Myrna, a Honduran Catholic woman, was married to an American Air Force Colonel who was also stationed in Japan. She said that one of her Catholic relatives in San Pedro Sula, Honduras, was converted to an evangelical by an "ugly gringo missionary with big ears." Gene knew that she was talking about his younger brother, Kenneth, who was a missionary at that time in San Pedro Sula - - Ha! Ha!

K.L.

Chapter 7

This chapter consists of pictures, letters and newsletters of our ministry in Mexico and Central America. God bless you richly for reading this autobiography and praying for this ministry.

TEXAS
1953-1968

TOP LFT: KEN, FRESHMAN AT
UNIV. OF TEXAS, '53
CENTER LFT: MOM, DAD & DEANY
CENTER RT: MOM,DAD,& SIBLINGS
AND MYSELF
BOTTOM: FOUR BOYS IN 1968

1954-1972

TOP LFT: KEN, COLLEGE STUDENT

TOP RT: 1961, GRADUATION
FROM SEMINARY (WITH
TWINS)

CENTER LFT: KEN AND DEANY,
1957, JUST MARRIED

CENTER RT: LINDA STOREY,
STAYED WITH US IN
GUADALAJARA, MEXICO

BOTTOM: LANGUAGE SCHOOL
CLASSMATES, 1972,
IN GUADALAJARA, MEX.

TEXAS,
MEXICO
AND
HONDURAS
1968-1977

"I'm Coming Stanley"

TOP LFT: FIRST TRIP TO OAXACA,
MEXICO IN 1968

TOP RT: MAN IN PUERTA VALLARTA,
MEXICO, RECEIVING THE
HOLY SPIRIT BAPTISM

CENTER LFT: PASSING OUT TRACTS
FROM BUS IN HONDURAS
CENTER RT: MAIL FROM TV PROGRAM
IN HONDURAS.

BOTTOM LFT: BUS ENROUTE TO
HONDURAS

TOP LEFT: KEN AND HAROLD WALKER
TOP RIGHT: KEN AND PASTOR REID
CENTER: PASTOR REID'S FLOCK
BOTTOM: AFTER SERVICES IN BRAES
         RIVER, JAMAICA

J A M A I C A
1970 & 1979

MEXICO AND HONDURAS
1972 - 1975

TOP LFT: ENROUTE TO MEXICO, 1972

TOP RT: HOUSE IN GUADALAJARA, WHILE
I WAS IN LANGUAGE SCHOOL
AND PREACHING IN VILLAGES

CENTER: HOUSE IN HONDURAS FOR THREE
YEARS, 1973-1976

BOTTOM: SUNDAY AFTERNOON SERVICE
UNDER OUR RENTED HOUSE IN
SAN PEDRO SULA, HONDURAS

GUATEMALA
1971 & 1980

PEOPLE GETTING FREE RIDE AT
EASTER TIME TO THE GUATEMALAN
BEACHES.

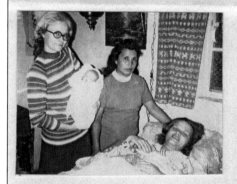

DEANY HELPING ANOTHER MID-
WIFE WITH ROBERTA ROVENSTINE
IN GUATEMALA CITY.

MAC BOYD AND GUATEMALAN PASTOR
AND FAMILY AFTER CHURCH SER-
VICE IN GUATEMALA CITY.

Christian Witness Crusade Faith - O - Gram

Kenneth Lowry
1206 Springrock
Houston, Texas 77055

October 1973

Apdo # 1019
San Pedro Sula
Honduras, C.A.

PRAISE THE LORD !!! God has richly blessed us all six here in San Pedro Sula. We arrived here on Saturday, August 17th. That first day we found a house (This is a miracle). We found out later that three other families had looked at the house and for some reason or another didn't want it. God gave us a nice four bedroom home on the side of a mountain for $100.oo per month (another miracle). We went to the International School to put our boys in school and instead of costing $250.oo per month, they asked Deany to be the school nurse which will more than pay for the tution. We con - sidered this for our first year until we get too involved for her to min - ister at the school.

We have been goning to the Catholic prayer meetings here on Thursdays. Recently we witnessed 30 young people receiving the Baptism in the Holy Spirit. We preached in a home out in one of the villages and saw two ac - cept Jesus as their Savior. God is blessing us more here than we have ever been blessed in our lives so far. A Pentacostal Catholic family have furnished our living room with all kinds of furniture. Praise The Lord ! Well, God is better than good, isn't He ? Keep us in your prayers that a real door of ministry will open to us here in a city of 130,000 people. God bless all of you precious Saints in the States.

In Jesus Love ,

Ken, Deany & boys

P S
"Anyone who would lke please send English or Spanish copies of "Run Baby Run " or "Cross &the Switchblade" etc could do so up to 22lbs per box This would be deeply appreciated

HONDURAS
1973-1976

SPORTS OUR FOUR SONS COMPETED IN
DURING THEIR THREE YEARS IN THE
AMERICAN SCHOOL IN HONDURAS.

TOP LEFT: DENNIS KEY PER-
FORMS OMAR AND
CONNIE'S WEDDING.

TOP RT: KIKE PANTING FAMILY

CENTERLFT: CARLOS PRADO AND
BRO. G.I. MCILVAIN

CENTER RT: CHURCH FELLOWSHIP

BOTTOM: ALVARADO FAMILY

H O N D U R A S
1973 & 1980

HONDURAS
1973-1993
TOP LEFT: RHINEHART FAMILY
TOP RIGHT: SALINAS FAMILY
CENTER LEFT: ALVARADO, MIR-
ANDAS, KEYS, BRO.
MCILVAIN
CENTER RIGHT: CASTRO FAMILY
BOTTOM: WERNER FAMILY

HONDURAS
1974
(May)

TOP LEFT: KEN ENROUTE TO A BIBLE
STUDY AT WERNER'S

TOP RIGHT: DEANY AS NURSE AND LIBRAR-
IAN AT INTERNATIONAL SCHOOL
IN SAN PEDRO SULA

OTHERS: CRASHED PLANE NEAR THE
SECO RIVER IN MAY, 1974

MISSIONARY REVIVAL CRUSADE
102 E. LYON ST., LAREDO, TEXAS 78040

PAUL KOEHLER
Calle Cuauhtemoc num. 187,
Tuxpam, Veracruz MEXICO
August 29, 1974

Dear Ken and Deany, and family,

Hi! Hope we're not misspelling your name Deany? We enjoyed your visit and trust t hat you will stop with us just as often as you can. How was your trip back to Honduras?

This is just a short note, since you already know the news here. We wanted to let you know that the Lord caused that $50 you gave us to grow real quick! Please use this for your television ministry, or, if you need it more elsewhe re, as the Lord leads. We got a check today for enough money to buy all the films we can use presently! So that verse you shared with us before breakfast was prophetic! We love you all. Our greetings to the boys, and brother and sister Alves.

In Christ,

Paul, Cheryl, + Kim
/ The Koehlers

Deany and I prayed that if the Lord would give us $500.00 by Monday, then she would not return to work this new school year as a nurse & librarian at E.I.S. (Escuela International Sanpedrana). The Koehler's gift came on Friday before the designated Monday! P.T.L. A gift of this size from another missionary on the field is a real miracle.

Thank You Jesus!

Ken
Ken Lowry

HONDURAS, 1974

THE AFTER EFFECTS OF
"HURRICANE FIFI" IN
SEPTEMBER OF 1974

CHRISTIAN WITNESS CRUSADE, INC.

1206 Springrock
(713) 464-9234
Houston, Texas 77055
United States

Apdo. Postal 1019
29 Av. S.O.#4
Colonia Figueroa
San Pedro Sula, Honduras

"Christians Witnessing unto Christ"

December 1971

Honduras is over the first wave of shock due to the hurricane disaster. From all general reports, about 10,000 lives were lost in the flooding and wind damage. About 53,000 people along the North Coast suffered damage to property, livestock and crops.

Many groups came to Honduras to help, such as the Red Cross, Care, Menonite Relief, Baptists, Catholics and others. We worked with practically all these groups in one way or another by sharing food, clothes and money sent to us by truck and mail from the states! The "free food" program has stopped and the men are being given a small wage plus food for their families in exchange for work in construction of houses or restoration of fields.

We have a television program every Sunday and want to have a daily 30 minute program as the Lord leads. Please pray with us for these daily programs. What Honduras needs more than anything else is God's Word which brings <u>real deliverance</u>. We were in a near-by city last week and a pastor told us of three people who accepted Jesus as their Savior due to the television programs.

God bless you real good this Christmas Season.
In Jesus'Love

Ken, Deany & Boys

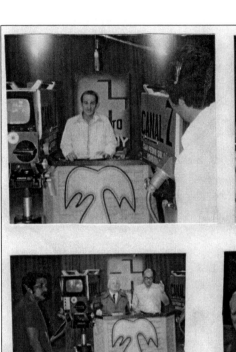

SAN PEDRO SULA, HONDURAS
TELEVISION MINISTRY OF JESÚS
CRISTO VIVE HOY (1974-1979)

BOTTOM: FIRST CONVERTS OF
TELEVISION MINISTRY,
JUANA, LESLY AND MRS.
HERRERA

TEXAS AND HONDURAS

BAPTISM SERVICES FROM
1974 and 1994

HONDURAS

1975

CAMPO MARATHON (SOCCER FIELD) CRUSADE
IN FEBRUARY IN SAN PEDRO SULA FOLLOWING
HURICANE FIFE IN SEPTEMBER OF 1975.

WE BELIEVED THAT
GOD WOULD SAVE
AS MANY PEOPLE AS
WERE KILLED BY
THE HURRICANE
WHICH WAS ESTIMAT-
ED AT 8,000.

Praise THE LORD

HONDURAS
1975-1976

EVANGELISTS AND MISSIONARIES WE
WORKED WITH WHILE IN HONDURAS:

TOP LEFT: JOHN HARRIS' GROUP
FROM SOUTH CAROLINA

TOP RIGHT: HAMMERNESS FAMILY FROM
CALIFORNIA

CENTER LEFT: JERRY NORMAN, NEW YORK

CENTER RIGHT: RAY ALVARADO FAMILY,
GEORGIA

BOTTOM: BOB AND CAROL CLARK,
OREGON

BELIZE   1975-1977

TOP LEFT: FIRST CONVERT IN BELIZE
TOP RIGHT: SCHOONER FOR MISSIONS?
CENTER LEFT:FERRY CROSSING
CENTER RIGHT:TENT REVIVAL IN BELIZE
BOTTOM: KEN AND PASTOR CASTILLO,
            SPIRIT-FILLED CATHOLIC
            PRIEST IN BELIZE HOLDING
            REVIVAL MEETINGS

CHRISTIAN WITNESS CRUSADE "FAITH-O-GRAM"

September 1976
1206 Springrock
Houston,Texas 77055

Priase the Lord!!

After arriving in the States the first of June, we spent
the summer making seventy video tapes for the television
ministry in Honduras as well as ministering in Texas,
Oklahoma, and New Mexico.

Two days before Deany's flight back to San Pedro Sula,
she awoke with a heavy blood clot in her right thigh.
Although she spent eleven days in the hospital, she is doing
fine now (P.T.L.) As we await our little girl's birth in
October, the four boys are enrolled in junior and senior high
schools.

By corresponding with Dennis and Paula Key, we are able
to keep in touch with the television, radio, and Christian
Center ministries in San Pedro Sula.

The Lord is allowing us time to build up ourselves in
the Word and various meetings while we are waiting upon the
Lord. So far He has told me this: "Run the race with
patience; the just shall live by faith; and keep the ministry
simple."

We appreciate the ministry to us as Deany was in the
Conroe "Doctor's Hospital recently. Also Thank You for the
prayers and praise you sent up to God on her behalf. God
richly bless you - in His Body- who continue to support this
small portion of His world-wide ministry.

In Bonds of Christian Love,

Ken, Deany and Boys

Kenneth, Deany and Boys
Hebrews 12:1-8

PTL TELEVISION NETWORK
CHARLOTTE. NORTH CAROLINA 28279

September 19, 1977

Mr. Ken Lowry
Christian Witness Crusade
1206 Springrock
Houston, Tx.   77055

Dear Ken,

Greetings from PTL! I received your letter and wanted
to thank you for writing and for your prayers for the PTL
ministry.

I truly enjoyed your visit and want you to know that
we are praying for you and your ministry. God bless you, Ken
and all that you do for Him. We thank you for your faithful-
ness to the Lord and we do covet your prayers.

In His love,

Sam Orender
Director
International Operations

SO/bc

M E X I C O
1968

JOHN CRAWFORD, TAKING A PHOTO OF DOUG MESSEL FROM OKLAHOMA AND
MYSELF AT THE AIRPORT IN TAMPICO, MEXICO IN FEBRUARY, 1968. A
YEAR EARLIER THE HOLY SPIRIT HAD TOLD ME TO BE IN MEXICO BY
FEBRUARY, 1968, BUT HE DIDN'T TELL ME WHERE IN MEXICO OR WITH WHOM.
WE FINALLY MET ROBERTO MORALES SALAZAR IN OAXICA AND MINISTERED WITH
HIM IN THE ISTHMUS OF MEXICO.

This letter was written from Mexico on February 28, 1968

Dear Deany and Boys,

We arrived in Veracruz and at the airport we met a missionary
named Douggan Thornton from Pasadena, Texas. He will take us
to Huiztla, Chiapas in his Dodge pick-up. We are trying to
let the Lord move us as He will.

Since I will not use all of my ticket (on Trans Texas Air) I
should get a refund on part or most of the $165.76 the ticket
cost. John (Crawford) thought I had the money for the
ticket; therefore there was a little misunderstanding and I
wrote a check at the airport. The Lord will provide. Please
write or call the bank and tell them if the check for the
ticket isn't covered, to please hold it for a week until I
return. God will provide!! Praise His Holy Name!!

Love to All,
Ken (Daddy)

Since 1997, Deany, other ministers and I have traveled to India, China, Europe, Africa, Australia and the Philippines. Maybe one day we shall gather our photos and newsletters and bring our readers up-to-date on some of these other 47 different countries. A good title would be "Not Many Mighty Are Called"!

If any home group, youth group or church family would like to have us share personally about missions, hopefully we can say that we have been in that particular country. We can be contacted:

Kenneth and Deany Lowry
1206 Sringrock Lane
Houston, TX. 77055-6313

Phone: 713-464-9234
Cell: 713-248-4456
FAX: 713-464-9234
E-Mail: cwitnessc@SBCglobal.net

POSTSCRIPT

Dear Friends,
    If you wish a copy of this book, write to us at:

To obtain additional books, please
call 1-866-381-2665 or on line at
htttp:/xulonpress.com/retailers.htm
or Barnes & Noble,Target or Borders

We will send you a soft cover copy of "Not Many Wise Are Called". The donations, if you wish to make, will be given, after expenses, to other missionaries whom we have met and who are currently building up our Lord's kingdom on this earth.

    If you would like for us to come to your home group or church congregation, please feel free to contact us at (713) 464-9234 (when we are in the U.S.) If we are not in the States when you call, please e-mail us at this address:

    cwitnessc@sbcglobal.net. Upon our return, we shall get in touch with you.

    Finally, if you are interested in our free Meditational Bible Digest Study, please read the following page for information. May our Lord Jesus Christ bless you richly!

Sincerely,
Kenneth and Deany Lowry
III John 2

CHRISTIAN WITNESS CRUSADE BIBLE INSTITUTE
1206 Springrock Lane
Houston, Texas 77055

Dear Serious Devotional Bible Student,

Several years ago C.W.C. began a new venture. We started a Bible Institute based in Houston to encourage believers to meditate on the Scriptures. At present we have students in Texas, Oklahoma, Zambia, Kenya and pending in other countries.

All students need for the Meditational Bible Study is a pen, loose leaf notebook and a Bible in their language. The study can be done in groups or individually. Students will read a paragraph, meditate on it, and then reduce it to one sentence on paper. The object of the study is to truly know the bible. The first session is Genesis through Job. The second session is Psalms through Malachi and the third is Matthew through Revelation. Upon graduation, the students receive a Diploma of Completion from C.W.C.B.I.

However, if students desire an Associate's college degree, they may receive an Associate's Degree from Liberty Theologicval Semionary in Houston (as long as this option is open). This Associate's degree must be done in college form; and there is a $50.00 processing fee. (Contact Dr. Frank Longino at 1110 Doral Lane, Houston, TX., 77073; 281 821-2407).

From 1988 to 1997, I studied for a doctorate in pastoral ministry (D.P.M.). From 1997 to 2004, I studied for a doctorate in biblical studies (D.Min.). In the last doctorate, I spent four years mentoring two students, meditating upon the Scriptures. The Meditational Bible Digest came from this study of the Bible.

If you are interested in the meditational approach of studying the Bible, please contact us at the above address, or email us at cwitnessc@sbcglobal.net.

Sincerely,
Kenneth W. Lowry, Founder
David R. Lowry, President

P.S. Here are a few Scriptures on meditation:

1. Isaac praying for a wife, Genesis 24:61 – 67
2. God commanding Joshua, Joshua 1:1 – 9
3. David delighting in Scriptures, Psalm 1: 1 – 6
4. Paul exhorting Timothy, I Timothy 4:11 – 16

Christian Witness Crusade

Bible Institute

Houston, Texas, United States of America

Confers this Certificate of Graduation to

Acknowledge the completion of the Genesis through Revelation

MEDITATIONAL BIBLE DIGEST STUDIES

upon

_____

On this_____ Day of_____

_____ Founder

Kenneth W. Lowry, B.A., B.D., M. Div., B.C.B.T., L.B.T., D. PM., D. Min.
Chancellor and Founder of Christian Witness Crusade Bible Institute

_____ President

David R. Lowry, B.S., M.S., P.E., D.D.

_____ Pastor

Christian Witness Crusade and Bible Institute
Kenneth and Deany Lowry
1206 Springrock Lane
Houston, Texas 77055-6313
U.S.A

Kenneth Lowry graduated from John H. Reagan High School in Houston in 1952. He joined the Merchant Marines for nine months for college money. Later, he attended the University of Texas from 1953 – 1954. It was in Austin at U.T, that God called him into the ministry.

In 1954, he was licensed by the Shoal Creek Baptist Church to preach the gospel. Kenneth was given a scholarship to attend Hardin-Simmons University, where he met and later married Earle Dean (Deany) Gandy, a nursing student from Hereford, Texas.

Upon graduation from Southwestern Baptist Theological Seminary in 1961, he pastored Baptist churches in Texas. Kenneth was awarded a Master of Divinity degree in 1973. Kenneth and Deany studied Spanish in Mexico for nine months before going to Honduras from 1973 – 1976.

Later, he was awarded a Doctor of Pastoral Ministry degree from Liberty Theological Seminary in Houston, Texas in 1997. Afterwards, Kenneth was awarded a Doctor of Ministry degree from Liberty in meditational Bible studies in 2004. From this study evolved the Meditational Bible Digest Studies that students are now studying in the U.S. and many countries around the world.

January 2008
Last trip – Honduras